HAUNTED
LIES

ELLEN NEWTON-DRISCOLL

HAUNTED LIES

Confessions of a *Former Ghost Hunter*

For my first hero, my father, Jack W. Newton.

From ghoulies and ghosties
And long-leggedy beasties
And things that go bump in the night,
Good Lord, deliver us!

CONTENTS

INTRODUCTION

I'M NOT SURE there was ever a time I didn't believe in the supernatural, the paranormal, the other world and the spirit realm, whatever one would call it. My brother, sister, and I were raised in a Christian home. My father is a retired Southern Baptist preacher. I was saved and baptized at age fifteen.

In giving some personal background I hope you will understand that I'm not only telling just another "ghost story." My hope is that you will understand I've been spiritual all my life. If you've read, heard or experienced something paranormal, I've had the sometimes dubious pleasure of experiencing those same things.

In November of 2009 I ounded Parker County Paranormal with a small group of paranormal investigators. We had some equipment, belief, respect for the work, and the best of intentions. Our goal was to treat people with respect, to never take money, and to help. We prayed in Jesus name before we left for each investigation, and we prayed with our clients.

In June of 2011 God told me in no uncertain terms to stop confronting entities. No one was more surprised than I was, except maybe my family and anyone who ever knew me. No, I didn't hear a voice though if I had, I'd have thought it a "way cool" experience, no doubt. Simply put, I found myself beginning to question why I was doing this. I'd never been doubtful before and pretty much "pooh poohed" my perceived views of what the Christian church thought about ghosts and anything paranormal. Many times I found myself defending and analyzing what my group did. Most of the time I defended before any question was even asked. I truly did want to honor God in everything I did, even ghost hunting.

My doubts began and wouldn't leave. To top that off, two friends and one family member came to me on three different occasions, without speaking to each other, and told me they were worried about me and my investigating. This would have made me mad at one time but now it only seemed to verify that God had an issue with what I was doing. After more thought and prayer I emailed a dear friend who I know would tell me not what I wanted to hear, but the truth. I'll never forget what she said.

"Old friend, I don't think you're supposed to confront anymore. Let the angels do that."

Talk about a brick wall falling on me. That was His message. I sat looking at the screen for some time. And so I told God that I heard Him, and I resigned as the head of Parker County Paranormal. It wasn't nearly as hard to give it up as it should have been, and from then on confirmation just kept coming. There was no doubt in me about giving up investigating. However, my husband, and co-founder of the group, had a bit of trouble with the whole thing.

God hadn't told *him* to give it up but again He didn't have to, really. Tom supports whatever I want to do, even if he may not always agree, and he did so again. My husband was very respectful of the fact that I was *absolutely sure* God wanted me to quit. And so he quietly quit with me. My young friend and her future husband had already begun to lose interest as they moved on to marriage and other life changes.

My son and his fiancé did not quit and only recently packed up the equipment for an investigation involving an old theatre. Before they went, I made them promise to pray and frankly worried the whole evening. They came back with no evidence at all and not even "that feeling" you get when something's off a bit. Or a lot! My son said it wasn't the same without me. I should have been flattered but the statement made me shiver.

Was I the one drawing out the things we'd seen or heard before? Was my "bring it on" arrogant attitude part of the problem? Maybe? Whatever one wants to call it, being sensitive, aware or "close to the veil" as my mother calls it, I am still that person. For me, at least, I became aware that I had to channel that part of me somewhere else.

First though, I'll try to explain what the study of the paranormal meant to me all of my life, and why I had to abandon something that had always been part of who I am. When I decided to obey the Lord completely and took myself out of investigating, a part of me was gone. Praying, I asked God, "All right but now what do I do with this? You made me. Surely there is something I can do with this part of my life."

This chapter of my life stalled for a while. I refrained from watching any television programs that even mentioned the paranormal. I didn't read my usual magazines and when a well-meaning relative gave me another book of ghost stories for my birthday, I thanked her and set it aside. Later she told me the look on my face said it all.

"I couldn't believe you were serious about giving up the whole ghost thing!" She said.

(Pardon the near pun, please.) But I was and what's more, it felt exactly right to avoid the same interests I'd always gobbled up before.

As I drifted during this time, I got a bit rebellious and decided I'd watch a very popular show I'd never missed before this happened. And I did, or I tried to. Nothing was the same; the thrill, if you will, was gone. I sat watching the investigators and *worried* about them. Did they really understand what they were interacting with? Were they in danger, real danger? These people were the professionals I had always admired. I didn't make it through the hour and turned the TV off. I felt as though I'd ended a relationship with someone I truly loved, tried to reunite with him/her but realized the love was gone, and nothing could bring it back. My heart and soul seemed in step with God's will for me, but my mind, my questioning mind, was in turmoil. At this point, I simply let myself drift, avoided what my heart told me to avoid, and waited. And waited. And then waited some more.

Months passed and gradually, I began to differentiate between what I could watch for the knowledge (still didn't know why I needed it) and what I had to avoid. The strangest emotion began to dawn on me. It was fear. Not an unhealthy fear, but the kind of fear we have as humans that preserves our lives. Though I have always been far from fearless, Lord knows I had not been afraid of the paranormal. Frankly I had always been proud of the times I went by myself into dark places and called out to whatever might be there with me. Proud! My group admired how I boldly marched into wherever, calling out to whatever. It was heady stuff, and I loved it.

Now "the scales had fallen from my eyes", and I knew I *should have* been afraid. For me, for my group, for investigators who boldly go where no one but the angels should go! At the very least I should have been afraid, and now am, for the fledgling ghost hunters who have no idea what they might be up against. Many have no or little experience with entities, as we did, and I believe are in danger if not for their very lives, their souls.

Now (and here's my shameless plug) let me tell you I have previously written three books but nothing like this one. My books are about the magical kingdom of Candlewood; the first one titled *The Dragons of Candlewood*. It was first published in 2006 and I'm very proud of it. Next followed *The Haunting of Candlewood* in 2008 and *Candlewood, The Legend of the Dragon Sword* in 2009. Before I even thought about the book you are reading I was finishing up the fourth book of that series, *The Crown of Candlewood*.

In addition I co-authored a book *When Christians Divorce*, with my Mom and best bud, Barbara Newton. She supplied the talent, and I supplied the divorce about 27 years ago. We hope it's helped those who find themselves in the terrible position of an "out of left field, this can't be happening" divorce. But my pride and joy is the Candlewood series about a prince named Kevin (my nephews' name) and his dragon named Fire. I tell people I'm a storyteller, not a writer and you may well agree.

I will freely, and honestly admit that I don't have the answers. I'm learning like everyone else, and I doubt any of us will know much for certain until we ourselves cross over. At any rate this book is the result of what I feel God wants me to do. He wants me to relate, not judge, but empathize through my shared experiences, and most of all, *warn*.

It is not my intent to belittle anyone or to tell any-one what God wants them to do. Your relationship with God is just that. Yours. But if you are an investigator, either professional or amateur, I urge you to bear with me and read on. I pray for your safety, your success, and your commitment in whatever you decide to do or undo. May God our Father protect you in all your coming and going.

CLOSE TO THE VEIL

ONE OF MY earliest recollections is of standing beside my sun-tanning neighbor, a Catholic lady, and listening to her tell me about guardian angels. She told me they went wherever we did and watched over us. I was enthralled and had a place set at the table for my angel for quite a while.

Then came my great interest in Mary, the mother of the Lord. While I'm sure that our neighbor must have told me about her I doubt she knew what influence she had on my young mind. The spiritual in life has always been a tangible part of me, even as a small child.

I became fascinated maybe even obsessed with Nativity or "Manger" scenes and began to put my own set together. My parents of course saw no harm in this, and one of my favorite memories at six years of age took place at our local five and dime store one December.

My manger scene had Mary, Joseph, and a lamb but no Baby Jesus. My parents and I looked high and low in that decorated store but no Baby Jesus. Disheartened, I remember getting into the back seat that frosty evening. My father just sat for a moment, gazing into the lighted Christmas window. Suddenly and without a word, he got out of the car and went back into the store.

I vividly remember seeing the sale lady's hand reach down into that display window toward the nativity set centered amongst the lights and fake snow. She picked up the Baby Jesus and placed him in my father's hand. Who was more pleased I'm not sure, but at age fifty four I still have that Jesus figure. He remains intact with his broken but mended mother, father, sheep, wise men, shepherds, angel, and donkey. The donkey arrived in my Christmas stocking that same year. My nativities number thirty-eight (at last count), but that one means the most to me.

When I was eight and my brother was five I wrote our first Christmas play. Produced and written by me, the younger kids were coerced into playing the parts. A red wagon decorated with ears was our donkey, and our audience was a more or less captive group of parents. Taking place in our basement, everything went well that first year.

When I was fourteen years old, we presented that play with some changes including using a real horse in our real barn. One year a friend suggested a Santa Clause play instead. Now, we all loved Santa, but we nearly had a civil war between actors and producers. Needless to say the Nativity play won out.

Somewhere in those years I remember a particular visit when my aunt and uncle, who were only two and four years older than me, came for their summer visit with us. These times were grand and much anticipated by all of us. We swam in our lake, watched movies, walked all over the woods and made fudge for no reason. We could hardly wait.

One summer, my scary movie loving uncle and I decided to try a "Ouija board." To this day none of us can remember whose it was and what happened to it afterwards. All I know is we decided to test it out and shut ourselves into a large closet with only a flashlight. My uncle began the questions and the answers were harmless enough. We were sure the other was moving the game piece, but we had great fun until my uncle asked "Who are you?" and everything changed.

I cannot or maybe choose not to remember whatever it was said to us, but we got an answer. This answer wasn't funny or "stupid;" it was mean. And it didn't come from either of us. The shocked look on Lonnie's face wasn't a put on, I knew. The dark seemed darker somehow, and it was with great relief that he proposed we stop playing. Hurriedly we put that board back in its box and as high on the shelves we could reach. We both told my mother what had happened. I remember her not being too happy. She told us to never play with it again. Looking back I imagine she got rid of it, but we never asked. She promptly destroyed it. And we never talked about what happened again.

*A quick note. I beg you, *never* buy or play with a Ouija board! Even in my ghost hunting days I counseled every client not to use them, and if they already had to destroy it. No exceptions. The Ouija opens doors that should not be opened, and those doors may not close again.

When I look back on my life I realize that this may have been the beginning of my interest in the dark side of the supernatural, the other side of the spirit world. Remember *Dark Shadows* with vampire Jonathon Frid? A friend and I decided to form our own fan club. We never missed an episode, and at that time, it truly seemed harmless and after I got a bit older, pretty silly.

Still between any Vincent Price movie and the Dark Shadows series and movies, well, my interest had changed more than I realized at the time.

I began to read books about ghosts and haunted houses. I gobbled up anything that had anything to do with the paranormal. Thinking back, I realize that was when my fear was being replaced with a nearly obsessive interest. Anything that gets rid of fear would seem to be a good thing, wouldn't it?

Maybe not.

ANGELS UNAWARE

THE FIRST ANGEL story I ever heard in regard to my family happened years before I was born.

My Uncle Alva and my Aunt Gladys (Giggy was her nickname, and we'll talk more about her later) lived in a little house in Mt Vernon, Illinois and had as long as even my father could remember. The building of Alva's new cement block garage was quite big deal to them.

One chilly day, Alva was burning brush. Somehow, the fire got away from him, and flames began to quickly spread to the garage.

As he desperately tried to fight the fire, a man in a white sailor suit, holding a ladder, appeared from nowhere and asked for a ladder. The stranger pushed the ladder into the garage causing the burning walls to fall. Soon the men had the fire under control, but the sailor made the difference. As Alva turned to thank the man for showing up just in time, he realized the mysterious sailor was gone. How he could have traveled down the long driveway so quickly and disappeared to wherever, Alva never knew. There was no reason for a sailor to be on that road on the outskirts of town.

So not every paranormal experience my family experienced was dark. I dare say most events were positive, helpful, and most likely life saving.

Years before my children were born I was driving somewhere in a little town in Illinois. I don't remember where I was going or why but I remember what happened.

For whatever reason, I looked down while driving. Maybe I was looking at directions. You'd think I'd remember but I don't. The next thing I do remember is the steering wheel being jerked out of my hands and the car making a hard right. Alarmed, I looked up in time to miss hitting a car coming straight at me. I had veered into the left lane and would have hit head on. I had to pull over and stop shaking for a while.

I did not turn the car. Heck, I wasn't even paying attention, much to my chagrin. Someone turned the steering wheel *for* me. Whoever it was saved my life. And this wasn't the last time.

A few years later my first husband at the time and I had lost our first child to miscarriage. This baby was much loved and anticipated. It'd taken us a while to even conceive, but at what should have been an ordinary appointment, my doctor couldn't get a heartbeat. Still she told me to go home. Maybe the date was wrong. I think I knew even then that it was no use.

I went home to bed rest but lost the baby at home, hemorrhaged, and had a dialation and cutterage (D&C). A deep depression set in. Had I done something wrong? What could I have done differently? All my thoughts were on my lost baby. My due date was March 7, and I held a grudge against September for taking my child.

One morning, I knelt on the floor in prayer, sobbing. How could I go on with such a broken heart?

Suddenly, I was aware of someone stroking my hair softly. The air was electric and still. My sobs began to subside at the sweetness of that touch. I dared not look up, but my heart felt more peaceful than it had in weeks. The strokes slowly went away, and I stayed there for some time in awe of what had just happened.

I know an angel was there, stroking my hair and comforting me. Healing wasn't over, but from that day on, I began to get better.

A year and some months later I told the Lord I could live without children if I had to, but He had to show me how. That same month I conceived Michael, and he was born in the much aligned September. He was a healthy nine pounder, and I was grateful.

Just as God works, He sent us Cody with no difficulty at all. We had just purchased a house. Michael was two, and we were trying *not* to have a baby for a while. God knew ahead how much his Momma and brother would need this little guy. Of course He was right. My husband left us in August, and Cody was born in November at only six pounds. He was the only light that we had in that black year, but what a light he was!

A few years later I was a single Mom and had a rare chance to go to a Christmas party.

The party was about thirty minutes away, and I started out alone around dusk. My boys were happily at their grandparents' house, and I was looking forward to the evening and some Momma time away.

I had just turned onto Hwy 35 in Fort Worth when a terrible apprehension came over me not to go. Puzzled, I couldn't think of any reason why and shrugged the feeling off.

Continuing to drive, the feeling would not go away. I turned around but at the last minute got back on the highway. *This is ridiculous*, I remember thinking. The feeling came back not to continue and to go home. I gritted my teeth and told myself to quit thinking about it and just go.

The third time the feeling was near panic and frantic. Go back! This time I couldn't ignore the message. No matter, I'd miss the party. I turned back and headed to Mom and Dad's house.

They were sure surprised to see me back and when I told them why, they were relieved that I had finally given in. Why it took me so long to "listen" to the message, I don't know. Believe me, when I get that rare, pure message now, I listen!

The messages didn't stop when we moved to Washington state.

Cody (at about age nine) and I were leaving a store parking lot, and we saw a young teenage girl with a sign. Whatever the reason, it breaks one's heart to see a young person with a sign. What could have gone to wrong so early in their life to resort to asking for money in a parking lot? You can't help but wonder. Cody saw her, too, of course. While we were waiting at the stop light, he quietly asked me if we could turn around. I knew what my sensitive son was going to do.

He'd received some money for his birthday and still had fifteen dollars left. That's quite a bit of money for a kid. At times, fifteen dollars has meant a lot to me, too.

Slowing to a stop, Cody rolled down his window and handed the young lady the money. She leaned in the window to thank him, and I think we both gasped.

This young girl had the greenest, loveliest eyes either of us has ever seen. Her smile would light up any room. There was just something *different* about her. Something unusual and unique. She didn't belong in this place and it was more than her youth and sweetness. We drove away silently, and Cody said it first.

"Mom, was she an angel?"

We truly believe she was.

Some years later in Washington, I landed a job at Hewlett Packard. One evening after work I was driving home and had stopped under the freeway bridge to make a left toward our house.

In my rearview mirror I saw a big work truck, not a semi but a not a pickup either, barreling down the hill and straight toward my stopped car. I don't remember being afraid but more accepting that I was going to get hit. Rather calmly, I wondered if I'd be hurt and how much this was going to damage my car. This all occurred in seconds, mind you.

Nothing happened and in the next second I looked out of my right window to see the truck still running and perched on the steep embankment. The driver and I locked eyes, and I could see he was as shocked as I was. How that truck came to a stop up there, I don't know. I don't think the driver did either!

After a slight exchange of waves, I turned left onto the highway and the driver slowly made his way down the hill. Did I see an angel? No, but something moved that truck. I suppose it could have been the driver, but there was no time at the speed he was traveling. And how did he make such a maneuver? To the day I die, I'll count this as a miracle.

One day I was at the post office in our little town. I had been to the bank to cash a check before that and was done with my errands. At least I thought I was.

As I walked out the door a middle aged lady approached me. She told me she had to get to a friend's house up the hill. She said she didn't have a car and didn't mind walking but she had asthma. Climbing that hill, and it was a very steep one, was out of the question for her. Would I mind giving her a ride?

I rarely give rides to strangers, and I was uneasy with her request, but I heard myself agree.

As she climbed into my truck, I realized I'd left my money envelope wide open on the console between us. Stories of being conked on the head swirled through me head but there was no help for it, she was in my car. We began up the long hill, and she kept telling me how nice it was of me to give her a ride. At the top I asked here where her friend's house was, but she told me to stop, saying this was close enough.

As she got out of the car she looked at me intently and said, "A thousand angels will one day come to your aid."

An electric chill ran through me, and I don't think I said anything to her. I started around the park square to go back to my house, but I just had to see where she'd gone. I circled back around to where I'd left her. She was nowhere around. I looked up and down the streets and through the park, but she was either one very fast mover (with asthma yet) or…she was something else. I'm going with *someone*.

Many years later after we'd moved back to Fort Worth, my oldest son, Michael, was in an accident. Being where he shouldn't have been at five a.m., he veered into the path of a semi truck, head on. The Jaws of Life got him out of the car, but people there knew he wouldn't make it. My mother called his cell phone, trying to find him, and a police officer answered his phone. The officer told my mother where they were taking Michael, and that we'd better hurry.

We all went together, totally in shock. I never saw my father drive like that.

When we arrived at the hospital, Michael's clothes were being cut off. He was as white as a marble statue, and his skin was cold. Blood was everywhere, and I could see one leg bone sticking out of his pants. A nurse quickly covered it, but I'd already seen it. To me, my son seemed dead already.

After surgery the surgeon told us he'd replaced a femur and an arm bone with metal. His sternum was broken as was his hand, and his spleen was damaged. He was placed in a medically induced coma, so we couldn't tell if there was any other damage to his brain. To our shock, we learned he'd had a heart attack. At age 22, my son had a heart attack, whether from blunt force trauma from the steering wheel hitting his chest or something else. He was in bad shape. To make matters worse, he developed phenomena on the third day just when we thought he might make it. All of us were numb.

Cody and I went outside for a bit, he for a cigarette and me for some air. We were sitting outside not talking when a homeless man approached and asked Cody for a smoke. He gave the man one and lit it for him. The man asked us why we were there, and Cody told him about his brother.

"Let's pray for Michael," the man said, and we bowed our heads and prayed.

The man prayed for Michael's healing with tears in his eyes. He uttered one of the most sincere prayers I've ever heard in my life. He told us he had to leave and "God Bless." We told him the same, and my son and I began to talk about how strange that was.

We decided to go inside the hospital the way he'd gone, but we couldn't find him.

It seems to me that the Olympic sprinting teams are missing out on the fastest people I personally have ever come across. Or perhaps angels come in all forms: green eyed girls, homeless men, or a firm voice in your ear.

Michael was in the hospital for sixteen days. His heart checked out as though the attack had never happened. His body healed in amazing time. So much so that the staff showed us his day to day x-rays. The progress was obvious. Told he would need a wheel chair or a walker, he used neither even for a day and a cane for only a while. While he wouldn't get to play football with the family that year, he did the next. At Christmas, my son stood next to me in church singing "Silent Night", and my heart was overjoyed.

As he recovered, Michael began to remember things.

He remembered hearing "Hang on, buddy. We're trying to get you out," as the Jaws of Life peeled back the top of the car. He remembered smelling gasoline and seeing how bright the stars were as the EMT's began to pull him gently out. Most of all he remembered a voice telling him, "Michael, Todd's here." Todd is an EMT friend of my brothers. He knew us, and he knew my boys. Later Todd told my brother he hadn't known this particular patient was Michael due to the blood, glass and injuries. When we told Michael what Todd had said he quietly asked, "Then who told me Todd was there?"

One day after the accident Michael sat straight up and said he remembered hearing my grandmother in the hospital. He told us she said, "It'll be okay, kid." (Everyone was "kid" to her.) My grandmother had been dead for a couple of years at that time.

Perhaps our 1,000 angels had been busy that night.

Sometimes you have to look carefully for those moments of comfort and joy. At other times they almost knock you down. Coincidence or "good luck" may not be that at all when you truly look at the situation. Be aware, for sometimes you "entertain angels unaware."

THE DARK SIDE

AT THIS TIME, I was a young single mother with two sons. If you had met me then, no doubt you would've thought school teacher rather than future founder of an investigative ghost hunting team. Believe me; I would've thought it was unlikely, too.

One not so good encounter with the unknown happened during the time the boys and I had moved into a little house in the Fort Worth area about a year before relocating to Washington. I remember it "felt funny" when we first looked at it, but the rent was right. We moved in, but we didn't stay long.

Though the days in the house seemed normal enough, the nights were something else. After putting the boys to bed, I slept fitfully in my own room. Most mornings found me on the couch in the living room.

At times we all heard noises, from the kitchen especially. Sounds like cups being set down on the counter were common. Sometimes we heard water running when the faucet wasn't on. Still, it was interesting but nothing "scary." Not at first.

One night, I was watching a movie when I heard something outside. Looking out the glass front door, the hair on the back of my neck shivered, and I knew someone was standing behind me, looking out too. It wasn't a nice feeling, and when I turned slowly around no one was there. My sons were sound asleep. Many things can be attributed to imagination, and I'm sure that's what I did that time. The next time I felt the presence it wasn't so easily ignored.

I had fallen asleep on the living room couch as was my habit, when I suddenly jerked awake. Someone had clawed my back, hard. I could almost feel the nails, but the worst part was the hatred I felt from my unseen roommate. I truly expected to see marks on my back, but there wasn't as much as a trace of a scratch. Whatever it was lingered for some time that evening, and I called my brother to come stay with us that night. Of all the paranormal things I've experienced this was and remains the most frightening. There is no way to convey the level of hatred I sensed. We moved out months before our lease was up and lost money. I didn't care one bit.

Several years passed between that incident and when Michael, Cody, and I moved with my parents to an old house in Washington. Too much water and too much paper keeps me from all the details that lead the five of us from North Texas to start a new beginning in Washington. My father began to pastor a little church in Vancouver, and I began work at Hewlett Packard. The boys started school, soccer, band, and football. When it seemed my brother in Texas might join us, we decided we'd look for a bigger place.

The newspaper ad that told of a wonderful, big house in the little town of Camas but none of us liked it at our first visit. Despite the space, the current atmosphere made a warehouse seem cozy. Back in the van our poor realtor hung her head and said, "What *are* you looking for?" We laughed but agreed that this house wasn't it.

Weeks and many houses later, I noticed the big house was still listed for sale. Should we look at it again? Reluctantly, my parents agreed to look at it once more.

This time the house looked *brighter* somehow. Flowers planted in the yard helped the overall appeal of the place, but something was definitely different. We made an offer, and despite a couple of hitches we moved in the fall of 1990.

On moving day several things happened.

Cody, four at the time, crashed his bike going down our new hill at break neck speed. A trip to the ER and five stitches later we arrived back at the house. Neighbor kids on bikes were watching the goings on, and one boy inched toward me and said, "You know your house is haunted, right?"

Now that's usually a conversation grabber but my attention was on Cody. It wasn't until later when Cody asked, "What does a haunted house mean?"

that I recalled what the neighbor boy had said. I don't remember what I said to Cody. I told my parents and we laughed albeit a bit uneasily, but it didn't really matter now. We were moved in, all three floors!

Everything settled in a routine, and Cody's fifth birthday in November came and went. Edwin, my brother, did indeed come to live with us much to our joy. The holidays approached, and Mom and I scrubbed every room. That was no small feat in a house with five bedrooms, two living rooms, two kitchens, a formal dining room and various assorted rooms, some of which had hidden doors. The house was an awesome place to play hide and seek! It was at Thanksgiving that Cody first saw something that kick-started nine years of life in a haunted house.

CHILDREN, SPIRITS, AND ANGELS

WE HAD JUST finished supper and were sitting around the dining room table talking. Cody, who had just turned five, left to go to the bathroom. To do so you entered the kitchen and turned right down the hall. The main bathroom was on the left, the writing room was on the first right, my parents room was the second right, the garage entrance was across from their room on the left. Directly ahead was the linen closet and laundry chute. Cody doesn't remember if he heard something or not, but instead of entering the bathroom he went to his grandparents' room.

The next thing we heard was Cody screaming as his little feet thundered back down the hall toward us in the dining room. I'll never forget what he said.

"There are three people in Mo and Granddads' room! A lady, a man and a little boy!"

Of course all of us were alarmed, and my brother reached the room first. Seeing nothing, he began to question his nephew. Cody insisted that not only had he seen three people, the lady had been sitting on the bed with the boy beside her and the man had been looking out of the window. Cody said the man had turned and looked at him. Upon reassurances that he'd only imagined what he'd seen Cody broke into tears stating, "I saw them, and no one will believe me!" I don't remember how we got him calmed down that night or even what we said after that, but it was the beginning of nine years of unusual happenings.

We didn't talk much about Cody's experience, but we had begun to notice some odd, small happenings in the house. The first any of us can remember to this day began with an old skeleton key. Somehow I'd lost my house key and as I'm wont to do, I was griping about it aloud. Taking my bedroom apart once more, I noticed an old brass key on my dresser. Nice, I thought but not the one I'm looking for. I did find my house key and went upstairs to thank Dad, who knows my love of old things, for the skeleton key. When I held it out and thanked him he said he hadn't put any key on my dresser and had never seen this one. Of course I asked everyone, but no one claimed to have seen it before, much less put it in my room. We shrugged it off as curious, and I have the key to this day.

After that, things began to happen more often. The daylight basement where the boys and I lived contained

a living room, a small kitchen, two bedrooms, a bathroom, several closets, a toy room, a laundry room, and
a room Dad used as his study. The rest of the basement
went back into the side of the hill the house was on and
had the usual basement things such as a furnace and a
work bench. There was a blocked off room under the
stairs. You could see the boards covering the opening,
but we never tried to remove them and see what was
there. We still don't know why we didn't.

I worked the night shift at Hewlett Packard, and one
day before the boys came home from school I walked
into the toy room to go upstairs. Stopping dead in my
tracks, I noticed that a few dozen little match box cars
were neatly lined up on the floor. No one was home but
Dad and me. The cars reached across the floor from one
end to the other.

Going upstairs, I asked, "Dad, did you line up
Michael's cars for some reason?"

"Huh?"

"Down in the toy room. Cars are all perfectly lined
up on the floor."

As puzzled as I was, he went downstairs to look.
There the cars were, as though a child had played and
left them.

"I didn't do this." Dad said. "Are you kidding me?"

"No, and they weren't there this morning."

We left the cars where they were and waited for
Michael and Cody to come home, but both were as
surprised as we had been to see the cars spread out.
We chalked up another odd incident and didn't worry
much about it. We told Mom and Edwin about it, but

they suspected the boys had done it and were either joking with us or had just forgotten.

From that time on, the experiences seemed to escalate.

Twice after getting both boys to school, I arrived home to cereal spread very neatly and deliberately on the downstairs living room floor. My sons hadn't done it. I knew because the last thing I did before getting them out of the house in the morning was to turn off the cartoons in that room and shoved both children out the door. Everyone else was gone, and although we all love a prank once in a while, I couldn't figure how this could be one. Nonetheless, I found that once was funny but twice vacuuming cereal up made this working mother a bit annoyed. I asked out loud for this to stop and it did.

My sister and her husband had arrived to spend Christmas with us, and the house was decked out in Christmas as is the Newton custom. Mom and I had decided to put them in my room and I would sleep on the downstairs couch. Taking their luggage down and chatting, I noticed that Linda's smile faded a bit.

"It feels kind of creepy down here, doesn't it?" she said.

"It does?" Though I'd always felt the same, I hadn't mentioned what I felt to anyone.

"It's fine, as long as I'm not down here by myself," Linda joked.

We dropped the subject, even laughed about it, and I made my bed in the living room.

That night was full of eating, talking, game play-ing, and more eating. Exhausted I excused myself and headed downstairs to bed. All comfy on the sofa, the Christmas lights twinkling and the sound of laughter upstairs, all was right with the world. I decided to read a while and snuggled into my blanket.

I was absorbed in my book when I saw something smoky white over the edge of my book, in the doorway between my room and the living room. Before I could even think and keeping my eyes on the page I remem-ber saying something like, "Don't appear, I don't think I can take it."

It was gone. Shaken, I put my book down. What had just happened? I didn't sleep much that night, but I didn't tell anyone about what I'd seen for a long time. Christmas continued on as it always does, and after a while I figured I'd imagined the whole thing.

We took about a hundred photos that Christmas, especially of Kevin, my seven-month-old nephew. Eagerly (no digital cameras, remember) I picked up our pictures from the pharmacy counter.

In several photos, most with Kevin as the main sub-ject, white, swirly, columns rose up and around him. Other pictures taken at the same time did not have these anomalies but the ones that did looked much like the white "swirls" that came down the stair case in *Poltergeist*. That's the only way I can describe them. No one was aware of them at the time, of course. Later I tried moving the camera strap into the lens and snap-ping some photos but those came back with the *black* strap clearly showing.

Cody took those photos to school once for "show and tell" but was ridiculed because the white columns "didn't look like ghosts" to the other kids. That soon helped Cody's decision to keep quiet about our haunted house and ghosts. Unless you have Casper on film, most people are disappointed by what the photo shows.

It didn't take me long to figure out that ghosts can be very different from what we might expect.

THE HOUSE

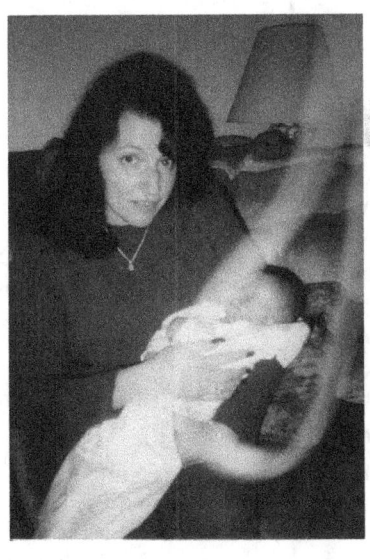

Ellen and Baby Nephew, Alexander in
our Washington Haunted House

MY BEDROOM DOWNSTAIRS, despite its "creepy" feel, really
was beautiful.

For some reason it was the only room in the house
with knotty pine walls and polished wood floors. My

wooden rocker and my great-grandfathers desk in front of a window made the room look like a little cabin. It was quite charming, but I couldn't sleep a wink. Even a night light, something I hadn't had since I was a child, didn't help. My eyes were drawn to the closet night after night. Turning my back on it was impossible, and even if I did the empty rocker bothered me just as much. I was embarrassed that such a pretty, big room could make me so uneasy. That is until a friend spent the night.

One night after an evening of games and movies, I offered her my bed, and enthusiastically made my bed on the sofa. Of course I didn't say anything about my room feeling strange. Frankly, I told myself it was just my imagination anyway. Deep down I think I wondered how someone else would feel sleeping in that room.

The next morning at breakfast my friend seemed quiet. When I asked her how she'd slept her answer gave me the chills.

"Not too well, really. You're going to think I'm crazy but I swear that rocking chair moved."

"Moved? You mean it rocked by itself?"

"Yeah, I swear it did. Something's wrong in that room."

If I needed verification, there it was. A room you can't sleep in isn't very handy though. It was my boys (I promise) who asked to switch with me. I know I didn't tell them *why* I didn't like my room, but somehow they must have heard enough to know I didn't like it in there. They thought it would be great, and since the room was so big they could take their bunk beds apart and cut the room in half. I made the switch with some trepidation. These were my babies! What if they got scared?

For many weeks after we switched rooms, I slept in the floor between their beds. They liked to sleep with their TV on, and I watched a lot of late night movies. Nothing unusual happened in that room for quite a while. In the meantime, activity in the house increased.

I began to have vivid dreams. In them I spoke with a man who seemed belligerent and loud, a woman in lavender who didn't say much, and a blonde headed young boy, around nine years old. He never said anything in my dreams, but I can see him to this day. He had old-fashioned clothes on and a "flat" sort of gray cap or hat on his head. In these dreams, the man monopolized the conversations. I don't remember what our conversations were about or if I even said anything at first.

One early Sunday morning as I dozed in bed, I felt a soft hand on my shoulder. "Go to church," a gentle woman's voice said. Somewhat irritated I awoke to tell my mother I didn't need her to wake me. No one was in my room, but the smell of perfume hung in the air, very slightly.

Puzzled, I went upstairs to find my mother in her recliner, Bible open sipping coffee. When I asked her if she'd been downstairs she said she hadn't, "Why?" I told her what had happened but my mother wasn't much of a believer in all things paranormal. At least then she wasn't. She laughed and told me I'd imagined it and probably had a guilty conscience since I hadn't gone the week before. It was then I noticed the perfume again, sweet and soft.

"Do you smell that, Mom?"

"What is that? Did you spray something?"

"No, I didn't. That's what I smelled in my room."

"Oh, it's nothing." And she went back to her reading. Case closed.

We smelled that perfume a couple of times in the future but it was never attached to anything bad. Years later we speculated whether the lady could have been an angel. At times we got the impression that there might be more than one type of paranormal activity going on in that house. Our suspicions were raised higher by something that happened one night after I picked Cody up from some sports activity or another.

Our house was built into the side of a hill, and you had to climb an even bigger hill and then travel down to get to it. It was full dark that night, and as we came over the hill and started down toward the house, I saw a white figure, at least man-sized walking around my father's van. We had loaded the van for a trip, and this entity was slowly walking around it. We both saw that it was a man wearing overalls with suspenders. Then he disappeared. I'm sure my mouth was open when Cody quietly asked, "Mom, did you see that?"

"Yeah, I did. Maybe it was an angel checking the van out for us."

"Maybe." Cody answered. He wasn't very surprised at seeing something, but he did seem glad to know I'd seen it too.

What I hadn't known until then was that Cody saw these beings all the time. He called them "white fades."

WHITE FADES
AND SHADOW PEOPLE

ACCORDING TO MY son he was around five when he started to see and hear the things he called, "white fades." Cody told us they were everywhere. He saw them frequently at school and said each child had one close by. They were in the cafeteria. They lined the playground and were even in the restrooms! Cody said he heard them speak sometimes, but he couldn't understand what they were saying and that it was "like you would hear someone behind glass, kind of muffled." Unlike the three dimensional, clothed people he had first seen in his grandparents' bedroom, these beings were different. He knew they weren't exactly human, but they didn't seem like ghosts either. The Bible speaks of beings of light as do many other books and articles I've read. White, light filled spirits? Angels would be my guess but not just by the way they look.

The white fades seemed to have a purpose. As Cody said each child had one. The school was full of them. Perhaps each angel has a child assigned to them? We don't know for certain but it would surely make sense that where children are, angels would be, too. And the white fade walking around our van? Cody and I both sensed that the man figure was checking everything out before our long trip.

As a family we're satisfied that Cody's "white fades" were, and are, angels. We may not be correct but no one can say for certain otherwise. We still take comfort in Cody's beings of light.

Unfortunately, he soon figured out that his friends and classmates didn't see the white fades, or if they did, no one said so. He learned to be careful about speaking of the things he saw. (And to not take ghost photos to school) But not all beings were white fades; of that he was certain. At times these other spirits appeared to Michael and Cody's friends as well.

One day the boys and a few friends were watching TV in the basement living room. Dad was outside, and I hadn't arrived home from work yet. As the boys climbed the stairs to go to the middle level of the house, they noticed the door at the top of the stairs was closed. This door was rarely closed, and there was no need for it to be most of the time. Michael turned the knob and pushed but the door wouldn't budge at first. Slowly the kids pushed on the door a little at a time until they could wiggle through. We had a portable dishwasher at that time, and you had to roll it from where it sat over to the sink where you hooked it up. Somehow the machine had been placed in front of the door leading downstairs! No one was in the house to pull such a prank, though my father might have if he'd thought of it.

Much questioning by the kids resulted in the answer. My father had not moved the dishwasher, and no one else was home. We tried to reassure the kids that if there was a ghost, it was a playful one. By then the occurrences had fairly convinced all of us (except Mom) that the house had another occupant. Mom might have been harder to convince but one night even she had to admit something was "up."

One night she came out of the boys room (formerly my room) after saying goodnight. As she walked through the toy room toward the stairs she made a comment about "the ghost" and laughed. To this day we talk about what happened next. Michael and Cody had several battery operated vehicles lined up on bookshelves. At that same moment every police car, fire truck, and ambulance turned on. Lights blazed on, and sirens howled. My mother jumped nearly out of her nightgown! Of course those of us in the room laughed until our heads hurt. We laughed even more when she determinedly jumped up and down trying to prove that walking across the room had caused the cars to go off. (It didn't work, of course.) It took a couple more incidents to make a true believer out of her, but she was well on her way after this.

Sometime later, my brother met and married a young lady from our church. At some point we all decided it would be a great idea if they moved in with us. We sure had the room! We moved Edwin and Lesa into the third floor, lock, stock and barrel. Dad's den was moved to the study room next to the laundry room. Lesa soon began to have nightmares and didn't want to be upstairs by herself at any time. We hadn't experienced anything on the third floor, but Dad's den had been the only occupied room. He had spent only limited time there. It wasn't long until our unseen visitor decided to be bolder with my sister-in-law.

One day Lesa was doing dishes in the main floor kitchen. She was gazing out the window when she felt a hand on her shoulder. She instantly thought one of us was home and turned, but no one was there. That was her first experience.

Later Dad moved his den from the house to an office at the church where he pastored. This meant that Cody, a new guitar enthusiast, could have the little room as a music room. There, in the basement area of the house, he could plug in his amps and play as loud and as much as he wanted. Most every day found him in the music room after school.

Lesa was scrubbing the tub on the main floor when she heard Cody strumming and chording in the music room. A vent from the basement lead right into the bathroom she was in so the guitar wafted in strong and clear. She had finished and was getting a drink in the kitchen when she heard the door from the garage open. The boys and I had taken the dogs out for a walk by the little river nearby and as the three of us walked into the kitchen Lesa's face turned pale.

"Did you just get home? All three of you?" She seemed very upset.

"Yeah, why?"

"Just come with me!" She took my hand and practically pulled me down the stairs. Michael and Cody followed. They were as puzzled as I was. Throwing open the music room door Lesas' mouth fell open.

"Cody, you weren't playing the guitar just now?"

Cody shook his head. "Why?"

Shaking, she told us what she'd heard. When my mother came home, we told her of course. Her reasoning was that our cat had somehow gotten into the room and run into the guitar. This made less sense than the ghost theory! The cat wasn't in the closed room when we came down, the guitar was upright on its' stand as usual, and we doubted "Gizmo" could chord.

By this time my pastor Father was convinced we had some sort of ghost in the house. He himself didn't like to be in the house alone, and too many items he'd put in plain sight seemed to vanish and turn up somewhere else. Also he admitted that he didn't like the boys room one bit. As he said, "You're never alone in that room." If nothing else this had proved to me we had an issue in the house. My father's attitude alone would have convinced me.

An electrical engineer and railroad man, Dad enrolled at the Baptist Theological Seminary in Fort Worth, Texas at age forty. The son of a preacher himself, I think he fought the idea that the son of a preacher was expected to become one as well. But years later, he was called by God. He, my mother, brother, and sister packed and left a married and newly pregnant me at the old home place in southern Illinois. It was a very hard move for them and only proved my father's devotion to do God's will. A person of common sense, not easily fooled but open-minded, I don't know a steadier man. For him to say he was uneasy at times in this house spoke volumes.

I don't remember why I was home one day, or if I was on yet another work schedule, but my father was a full-time pastor at this time. He was in and out of the house with no set schedule, and so one day I glanced up the stairs as I was cleaning and saw my father standing at the top of the stairs. I called out, "Hi, Dad," but got no answer. Wondering if he hadn't heard me, I backed up and looked up the stairs again. No one was there. I went upstairs but no one was in the house but me. Later, I remembered thinking that the "form" I thought was Dad was dark. But when a person sees something out of peripheral vision it's often not until later you realize something wasn't right.

At the time, there was only one paranormal television program that I remember. Psychic Peter James hosted, and I wondered on more than one occasion if we should contact him. Still, admitting your house was "haunted" at that time met with more than a snicker or two. We told very few people and only if they felt, saw, or heard something. Some shared stories of paranormal experiences they'd had personally. It surprised me that so many different people from different walks of life had some of the same experiences in common. Some were Christians, some weren't, but many of the stories they told were similar. The only thing a person could do was confide in someone who wouldn't laugh at you or call you crazy. The ghost hunting frenzy we see today hadn't yet begun in earnest.

When I worked at Hewlett Packard in Vancouver. I made many friends there, and one of those I remember for her kindness and her smile.

On my first, very nervous, day there I was assigned to work on a particular assembly line. While most people were nice enough it was hard to become part of a team of strangers. One young lady, someone I'd call a "hippie chick" turned from her station and smiled a brilliant smile at me. She introduced herself, and we became instant friends. It soon became apparent this she was much loved and a friend to all. We talked about many things, and if I was lucky enough to work next to her the days passed quickly.

We had several shifts at the plant, and she transferred to an evening shift while I stayed on my daytime shift. I missed our talks but we'd pass at times with a "Hi, ya old lady" to which the other would respond, "Hi, ya old bat!" She had a devilish sense of humor.

I came in one morning and noticed how quiet the place seemed. People were gathered at the end of the production lines, talking softly.

My friend, Linda, met me and asked if I'd heard what had happened the night before. I didn't know what she was talking about. Our friend had left work after her shift bound for home. A drunk driver hit her car, and she had been taken to the hospital where she died from her injuries.

Our plant was devastated. She left two young sons about the same ages as my own. She'd just taken a trip to the beach and had berated herself for spending the money. It didn't matter now. Many people attended her memorial service. It was nearly impossible to believe she was gone, and the last we saw of her was a portrait of her at the beach only days before.

I don't remember how long she'd been gone when the following happened, but I do remember that Linda told me she'd felt "cold" at the end of her production line. Our friend usually met us there to talk and gossip. Still, we didn't think much about a cold spot.

One day, I was in the cafeteria on break. I was looking at the menu trying to decide which poison was better for me when I heard, "Hey." I turned around to say "Hi, ya old bat" before I realized it couldn't be my friend. No one was there, and not one person was in that part of the cafeteria either. I know what I heard, and my first response recognized the voice. Was it she, my friend, or wishful thinking on my part? I never heard the voice again.

Another day I was quickly walking down a corridor to fetch some parts. I heard something like a "bee" or a buzzing sound in my left ear. That's as close as I can describe it. Later, I read about time crossing or rather crisscrossing and that perhaps the sound I'd heard might be attributed to that. I simply don't know, but I've never forgotten my friend.

My house and its strange happenings made for many a conversation, especially at work.

One evening, a young lady asked me to describe my house. Listening intently, she became very excited and exclaimed, "I know your house! I've stayed the night there many times when my friend and her family owned it!"

Without saying more I asked her what she remembered.

She told me the "cereal on the floor" event had happened many times, and that she and her friend had borne the blame for that one more than once. I laughed and told her I could certainly vouch for her if she needed me to!

The knotty pine paneled room was the second memory to come to her mind. None of that household liked the room, either, despite it being the loveliest and biggest bed room.

Although she mentioned the little boy and the belligerent man, she said nothing of the perfume lady. Talking later, we both mused why the previous family hadn't seemed to see or hear her. We both agreed that the first floor daylight basement was key somehow.

It comforted us greatly to know we hadn't been the only ones. Soon, we discovered the house's other occupants had shown themselves to others as well.

IT'S A SPOOKY DAY
IN THE NEIGHBORHOOD

ONE DAY, OUR neighbor lady next door came over and point blank asked, "Has anything weird happened in your house since you've moved in?" I remember inviting her in eagerly. Maybe, just maybe, other witnesses affirmed that my family wasn't collectively insane after all!

She proceeded to tell me that the former owners were friends of hers and had asked if we had experienced anything in the house. So, my young friends' story wasn't the only one it seemed. My neighbor told me that not only was our home haunted, the entire hill itself was! Apparently a man died in our house, in the very room that caused so many uncomfortable feelings. (Now my sons' bedroom) Okay, many people died in houses so that didn't particularly alarm me. My own grandfather had died in my grandmother's house, and nothing felt strange or different there. We'd never had any strange things happen there. But what she told me next made the hair on my neck stand straight up.

Her own house had "something dark" in it, she said. A man, a dark man, in her basement. Something bad had happened in the house, but she didn't have all the facts. Up the hill as you left our street, another house was the sight of a fire of unknown origin. Apparitions, she said, were seen there often. One neighbor, a Native American told her that she herself had experienced paranormal sightings and heard things in her house as well. I remember sitting back, trying to soak it all in.

The James River flowed just below our houses at the bottom of the hill. I remembered reading that flowing water seemed to be a factor in some hauntings. Were these events part of something occurring naturally?

In some way, my neighbors words gave me hope. We weren't the only ones who knew their homes were different, and maybe these things could be explained through nature somehow. When our neighbor called the previous owner back to let her know we had indeed seen and heard things, the lady had burst into tears. Our neighbor said the poor lady kept repeating, "I'm not crazy, I'm not the only one." Her relief was apparent, and I felt badly for her. I've since wished we'd met and compared notes, but we never did.

For a little while I felt better. That changed when things in the house got even worse.

Another neighbor's husband became very sick. Soon, it was apparent he wouldn't live long. My father tried to talk with him about what lies in store in the after-life, but he was not interested. He was a very nice man and a great neighbor. We missed him very much.

Weeks after his death, I was downstairs in the toy room, moving bookcases. From my bedroom to the right of the staircase I heard, "Elllleeennn…" Every hair on my arm, head and neck stood up. Slowly, I entered my room already knowing no one was there. I checked everywhere downstairs just to confirm that no one was on that level of the house. Shaken, for I'd never heard my name whispered like that, I went upstairs. When my funny mother told me I "looked like I'd seen a ghost" I told her I hadn't but I had *heard* one say my name.

Even now I remember that the voice seemed strained, as though coming from some distance or that speech was difficult for him. That was the one thing of which I was certain. The voice was a man's voice. I had no proof of any kind, but I couldn't help but wonder if the voice was my neighbor. Whoever it was, he knew my name. That fact bothered me more than anything paranormal that had happened to me.

Though the future held more strange events for me, this occurrence is the one that stands out not as the most frightening but as the most disturbing. There's something truly unnerving about an entity knowing *your* name, but you don't know *their* name. When I remember this event today I am as disturbed by it as I was at the time. Then, I wondered who it was. Now I wonder what it was. (Later this experience would give me my belief statement. "I know ghosts *are*, but I don't know *what* they are.")

Meanwhile, events in the house continued.

As I stated earlier, my sister-in-law lived on the third floor with my brother. Often times she would find one shoe of a pair missing. Inevitably, we would find the shoe on the first floor in the toy room. Usually, the missing shoe was found at the bottom of the stairs. That became so common she would call my phone downstairs and ask if her shoe was there before she looked anywhere else! As funny as that might seem, it bothered her a lot and whatever walked there seemed to delight in scaring her the most.

Michael had a white kitten named "Gizmo." Because of her antics I began to collect anything with a white cat on it. My kitchen was full of white cat teapots, white cat kitchen towels, magnets, figurines, and many other things white-cat-related. As I've explained earlier our house had several odd rooms and empty spaces. One day when I was hanging up some of the boys jackets for the millionth time I noticed that there was a space behind the high shelf. This closet backed the boys' bedroom closet. Why there was a space between the two is anyone's guess, but there it was. I got a flashlight and peered down into the space, which reached all the way to the floor.

There at the bottom of the space was a big, plastic white cat! Puzzled, I called Lesa down and had her look, too. There it was, a white plastic cat. How in the world we'd get it out we didn't know. She left me to my musing and went back upstairs. I had other things to do and just left it for later.

I went into the boys' room to hang up more of their vast wardrobe. Turning on their closet light, I nearly jumped out of my skin. There on the shelf was the plastic white cat. Immediately, I called Lesa down, and together we looked in the first closet. The cat wasn't there. Back in the boys closet the cat still sat and Lesa noticed another thing. Cobwebs and dust on the cat hadn't been disturbed. If someone somehow had reached down and pulled the cat up from the space between the closets, wouldn't the dirt and webs be partly gone?

We backed out of the closet and shut the door. As each person came home we called them in the room, told the story and showed them the cat. Even Mom had no explanation for it. Finally, I decided the cat must be a "gift", and taking it down I cleaned it up where it sat in on my kitchen bar for a while. However, my sons didn't like it very much, and soon it was relegated to a shelf in the basement. I hoped I hadn't insulted someone.

Despite the dishwasher in front of the door incident, our house was always full of extra kids. Part of the reason might have been that Michael and Cody had a mother who took kids out for ice cream or cheeseburgers a lot, but another was because the house really was a lot of fun to play in. My brother added to the fun by bravely hiding in the basement and chasing the kids with a rubber hatchet. My black lab usually followed, barking and nipping my brother in the behind if she thought he was being *too* scary. One day, one of their best buddies ran up the stairs. I'll never forget how pale he looked.

"Miss Ellen, there's a boy down there."

I remember thinking, *What else is new?*

"What boy?"

"In the mirror, behind me. I was combing my hair, and he was behind me watching. When I turned around, he was gone."

Cody had seen the little blonde boy years before when we first moved in, and I'd even dreamed of him but this was new. Downstairs I found the rest of the crew chattering excitedly. None of the others had seen him, but they believed their friend. One of the other boys seemed quiet, and when I asked him what was wrong he said, "I've seen him, too. He was outside and I saw him through the guitar room window. He was looking in. I didn't want everyone to think I was weird."

When I asked this boy what the blonde boy was wearing he described exactly the same clothing and hat that the other friend had already told me. Blonde, about nine, shorter than them they agreed, with suspenders and a flat, gray hat. He didn't say anything, and even in my dreams he was silent.

Now I gave birth to sons. I know "boys will be boys", but I also am fairly savvy about boys lying and these boys, in my expert Mom opinion, were not lying. The fear I saw on one little face that day was no put on. Cody had been right all along. One of the "ghosts" was a little boy. I cannot convey how badly I felt for this little lost boy. Why would a child become a ghost? Did God just leave children to wander?

My belief system slipped a bit that day, I'll admit. It took years and more experience before my heart and mind became at peace over the subject of ghost children.

WHOSE HOUSE *IS* THIS?

MY DREAMS CONTINUED. The belligerent man as I called him, the lady in lavender, and the little blonde boy visited me, but as always only the man talked. Mostly he shouted at me, but I could not remember when I woke up what he was telling me. I began to think it was his presence that we felt in the boys' room. Not necessarily evil, but pushy, bossy, and unpleasant. But as time went by, the man became more insistent.

Michael told me that he woke one night and a man was standing in the doorway. I quickly told him it was his Granddaddy checking on them. I didn't know if that was the truth or not when I made that statement. After speaking with Dad, I knew it wasn't but for my son's sake, we let the lie stand. Was the belligerent man watching my children? At this point, I knew he wasn't anything good or comforting.

I began my old habit of sleeping on the floor between the boys' beds.

One night, I was watching TV in the room. Both boys had drifted off. Suddenly, I heard Cody's guitar chording up and down, up and down. I actually got to my feet and went to the guitar room door. The chording continued, and I put my hand on the knob.

"Please stop," I heard myself say. "You'll scare the boys."

The music stopped.

When I went back into the bedroom Cody was sitting straight up.

"Mom, I heard my guitar."

"No, honey, it was the TV. I checked."

Cody lay back down, and I was unhappily reminded that I had lied again to one of my boys.

One night (back in my own room) I was dreaming again of the three spirits. This time however I was afraid of the belligerent man. And in this dream, I spoke, interrupting his tirade.

"In the name of Jesus of Nazareth, leave this house!" I heard myself say.

"But my name is…" The man shouted and vanished.

I woke up and thought two things. One, what was his name, and two, I knew the house was better. What I didn't know was why I had said those precise words in my dream. Casting a demon or spirit out in Jesus' name was something I'd heard and read of, but I hadn't known exactly what words were used. Years later I discovered that part of the Catholic exorcism ritual includes the words "in the name of Jesus of Nazareth, depart from this place."

Maybe I read that somewhere. Maybe I'd heard those words from someone. Maybe it was for my own safety that I wasn't to know the spirit's name. But I'll go to my own grave swearing I did not know any part of the exorcism wordage. At least my conscious mind didn't.

The downstairs atmosphere felt better now. When my sister, her husband, and family returned that year for Christmas, she commented, "Your room feels way better."

Still, the activity continued but more often on the third floor. My brother and sister-in-law had my nephew, Alexander, while they lived with us. Like any newborn, he didn't sleep all that well during the night.

One early morning, my brother felt someone shake his shoulder to wake him. Being a new daddy, he'd just returned to bed and dozed off. He ignored the hint but again, he felt someone shake his shoulder. This time was a bit more insistent. He awoke and jumped out of bed. His first instinct was to check on baby Alex. He was fine, but we've always wondered if maybe he *hadn't* been. This was one of only two experiences my brother had, despite his defiant "I dare you" out loud remarks.

When Alex was two months old, my brother got a job offer in Texas in a little town called Azle. He'd worked for this newspaper before and was offered the job of editor. His little family reluctantly left the boys and the rest of us in Washington and moved back.

At this point I'd have done most anything to make my boys happy again. They and my brother were (and are) very close, and they missed him terribly. I had to do something to help them get through this change.

It occurred to me that the third floor was now vacant. It had two bedrooms, one on each end with another room between them. Lesa had gutted part of the attic and made a huge closet. Each boy could have their own room and their own living room between them. It seemed perfect, and the idea of getting them out of their present room, better or not, felt good.

Dad had missed having his own office back in the house and agreed to move his things back into the boys' room downstairs. He wasn't too uncomfortable in that particular room anymore. The only thing I didn't like was that most of the time I'd be on the first floor alone. But again the atmosphere down there wasn't nearly as heavy as it had been. And the boys were ecstatic. I thought things were settling down in any case.

One day I climbed up one flight of stairs from the laundry room and then took the stairs that led to the third floor. I had my arms full of clothes as usual. Both of my sons seemed allergic to putting clothes away. At that time, I was way more concerned with such things. All three of us got over it.

My first stop was Michael's room on the left. As I entered the room with the over-flowing basket, I saw it again. The white fade, as Cody would call it, was simply standing beside Michael's bed. This time, however, it appeared to be shorter. My response was funny even to me.

"Oh, hello." I said.

No sooner had I said the words when it vanished in an instant. I simply stood there and looked at empty space for a minute. It was my first encounter with anything on the third floor. I'd thought that part of the house was fairly quiet, ghost wise. After talking to the boys about what had happened I learned I was dead wrong.

Although Michael hadn't experienced much personally, other than the door being blocked with the dishwasher, Cody had experienced many things both in the house and out. Most of what he'd seen or heard seemed harmless or unaware of him. But the story he told me about what had happened in his room chilled my heart.

Cody never had slept well, and this particular night had been no different. As he tossed and turned he "felt" something under his bed. Peering down into the blackness, he saw something crawl out from under his bed. It crossed his room, rose up, opened the door and then closed it.

Open mouthed because I sure hadn't heard this before, I said, "Cody, what did you do?"

My son looked at me in all seriousness and said, "I went to sleep. I think it was keeping me awake."

As I recall Michael and I just looked at each other. I know my respect for Cody went up ten notches, and I'm betting Mike's did, too. Not at my bravest could I go back to sleep after something crawled out from under my bed!

That night we hung two big glow in the dark plastic crosses; one in Michael's window and one in Cody's. It made me feel better at any rate. Neither boy expressed an interest in leaving their floor, and I had to hand it to them. As Cody said, "It didn't hurt me." I remember wishing I felt that secure about it. But after all, these were my children. Any parent knows what I mean.

Many times I've heard or read that animals are very sensitive to spirits. At this time we had two dogs, one in the house and one mostly outside and Michael's white cat, Gizmo, who pretty much refused to go outside. Our white sheepdog, Yoda, preferred the outdoors, and I don't recall any situation where she was involved in anything supernatural.

Gizmo, however was another story. She stared sometimes, her tail lashing, at the ceiling. We of course could see nothing, but whatever she saw seemed to stir her up. At times she would utter that low growl deep in her throat. Other times, she would simply meow at whatever it was. One time I saw her standing on her little cat legs and batting at something. She was on my bed at the time, and what she saw was directly over my pillow. *Of course it would be my bed*, I remember thinking wryly. But at least she seemed to be playing with... whatever it was.

As strange as that was, nothing compared to the way the house and its' secret affected our black Lab, Rainey.

RAINEY THE "TURTLE"

RAINEY WAS SUPPOSED to be a turtle. At least that's what my mother points out to this day.

Cody wanted a turtle. I thought it a reasonable request and knew just where to look for such a creature. Michael, Cody and, I got into our truck and headed to our vet's office to look on the bulletin board there. We hadn't seen any box turtles like my brother and I used to catch back in southern Illinois, and for all I knew Washington state didn't have any free turtles for my son.

We weren't there for five minutes when one of the ladies there said, "Hey, are you maybe interested in a black lab puppy about ten months old?"

I remember opening my mouth to spit out a stern "NO" when the sound of paws on formica flooring hit our ears. A smallish black pup skidded around the

corner and planted herself at my feet; her brown lab-
bie eyes looked up into mine. I was defeated. The boys
were delighted. Grumbling and shaking my fist at the
giggling technician, we left the vet's office with Cody's
"turtle."

It was one of the best decisions I ever made.

Rainey immediately ingratiated herself to everyone.
My mother, however, was harder to convince and kept
repeating, "But you went to get a turtle..."

Soon it became apparent that the little black Lab
was very special. Even Gizmo liked her. The little white
cat didn't like many people and considered any other
animal beneath her. I still have a photo of Rainey and
Gizmo, black dog and white cat, happily snoozing close
together on my blue bedspread. Yes, Rainey loved everyone. Most everyone that is.

No one remembers what the occasion was or why
we were all in the dining room together instead of the
kitchen, but everyone remembers what happened the
first time Rainey met "the other people" as we referred
to the ghosts. We were all laughing about something
when Rainey began to growl. We weren't certain she
could sound like that, but she did this time. Every
hair on her back raised, and she crept slowly into the
kitchen, looking down the hall. No amount of coax-
ing would calm her, and finally my brother went down
the hall.

As usual nothing was there that we could see, but
Rainey was in a state and wouldn't even look at us.
Despite our reassurances that it was "okay" and no one
was there she stood stock still in the hallway for some

time. Finally, she sat down and stopped growling. My sister-in-law and I sat beside her for some time until she finally relaxed, wagged her tail and left to play ball with the boys and my brother. That was her first experience but it wasn't her last.

We found out another strange thing about Rainey.

My parents had invited a couple they knew for coffee one evening. Rainey and I came into the room to say hello but the dog would have none of it. Rainey growled so much I had to apologize to and remove her. Never had she behaved like that before, and we were all bewildered until my best friend came over one evening. A dog lover, my friend was heartbroken when Rainey would not come near her much less be patted. This was very strange. Rainey had always liked everyone she met until now. Then it occurred to me one day.

The couple my parents had over had white hair as did my friend. For whatever reason, Rainey did not like anyone with white hair. I encouraged my friend to come over again, and with time and much soothing Rainey learned that this person had treats and was okay. After that, Rainey met her with much tail wagging and kisses. For years since my family and I have wondered about Rainey's real dislike of white hair. It's occurred to us that maybe, just maybe, she connected white haired people with the spirits in the house.

A few times I came into my room to find Rainey looking intently at the ceiling over my bed. I'd seen Gizmo do the same, her tail swishing back and forth, her eyes unblinking. It took a few moments and pats to break the spell each time. It took longer than I can remember but Rainey either accepted what it was or saw different entities in the house. At times she would wag her tail, sit and apparently be patted on the head. Now that was freaky. Other times she became still, her eyes glued on whatever she was seeing but her growling stopped, at least during the day light hours. Gizmo never seemed to warm to what she saw and I think ignored it for the most part.

All bets were off if it was nighttime. Rainey stuck to me like glue. I remember it was hard to make my way upstairs because she stayed so close to my legs. This habit was much worse at night. The boys often tried to make her sleep with them, but she would have none of it. Somehow I think she knew her place was with me, downstairs. It was very disconcerting to wake in the middle of the night and see my dog's profile in the darkness as she sat on my bed next to me, growling that low, guttural sound she made when something wasn't "right." Later I figured I would never know how this loyal, loving dog had protected me. And from what.

Rainey suffered from parvo soon after we took her home. The vet's office had been told she'd had her shots, but she hadn't. Her life hung in the balance for days, and everyone who knew her, including Dad's church, prayed for her recovery. Finally, the vet had given up in tears and we took her home to die with us. We took turns gently forcing her to drink Pedialyte because she would not eat.

One day I came home from work and headed downstairs to take over for Dad. There he lay on the floor next to Rainey, stroking her and praying. I'll never forget his words.

"I know she's just a little dog, Lord, but we need her. Please let her live."

It broke my heart to see my father's face streaked with tears for the sake of this pup. I took over my turn, and there we slept on the floor, until I had to go to work the next day.

In the stone ages we carried "beepers" not cell phones. I was on the production line when mine went off. The house number came up and my heart sank. Surely Rainey had died and I wasn't there with her.

Dialing the number my fingers shook, but when Dad answered the phone I was surprised at how he sounded.

"Rainey ate pizza crust! I just gave her some, and she ate it!" He was ecstatic.

When I got home I found a much better Rainey and a relieved family.

"Prayer, pizza and Pedialyte!" Those were the words my father used to describe her healing.

The vet had warned us that even if Rainey did survive, the illness had taken years off her life. We didn't care. Like my father said, "we needed her."

We got to keep her for nine more years and she, Yoda and Gizmo made the move from Washington back to Texas with us. Rainey began to suffer seizures, and we spent a horrible two days trying to give her medication our vet had prescribed. He was sure we could get them under control, and that she could live several more years. Rainey's last night was horrible. The seizures wouldn't let her sleep, and she continually bumped into furniture, seemingly unaware of us. We had previously prayed for her to live, and now we prayed for her to die. As soon as the office opened I called our vet who told us to bring her in. He would try a different medication.

Dad covered Rainey in a blue blanket, and my mother, in tears, ran to the car with Rainey's favorite "baby" to take with her. My mother said she and Rainey had become "two old ladies together."

Two hours later our vet called and told us he couldn't get the medicine to work unless he took Rainey off the tranquilizers. Unfortunately, each time he did the seizures returned in full force. I remember what he asked me. "What do you want to do?"

I wanted my dog to return home. That's what I wanted, but I knew she wouldn't come home alive. We climbed into my car to be with her. Mom began to call family members to tell them each what was happening. Most asked that we "wait until I get there" before we let her go. My oldest son couldn't take off work and told me through his tears what to tell her for him. Eight people sat on the floor with her while the vet gave her the drug that sent her on. We took her home and put her in the back room of my parents' house while the men dug a grave for her under some pine trees. One of my nieces and a nephew came to the house and patted her good-bye. I don't know which of us was more inconsolable.

In the days that followed, we thought we heard her. We heard her collar jingle or we would hear her climbing the step of the RV we lived in while Tom went to school. One time my husband heard her "woof" before he remembered she was gone.

Coming up my parents drive one afternoon, I saw a black dog out of my peripheral. It was sitting in front of the far fence in Rainey's "spot." I practically slammed my brakes on but when I looked again, there was no black dog. Wishful thinking? Maybe. Was she there while we grieved, staying to comfort us as best she could? Perhaps.

Maybe three years later we had gathered at my parents' home to watch a movie. I saw a dog walk across the floor in front of the entertainment center where Rainey's bed used to be. What I actually saw can only be described if you've seen the "Predator" movies. When the alien was "cloaked" and hiding in the trees, the soldiers could make out "something." What I saw was the outline of a dog but the mass of the body looked blurry and see through. That's as close to a description as I can get, and I've not seen anything like it again. None of us have heard or seen Rainey in a long while.

I don't know what happens to our animal family members after death. Or at least I can't prove anything. I personally feel that Rainey lives on in Heaven. The Lord made animals first, after all. The Bible says He knows every sparrow that falls and knows when each deer gives birth. I know He let Rainey live nearly ten more years. Maybe there are times when God allows certain things to comfort us.

Some people feel that God sends angels "disguised" as our loved ones or angels posing as animals! Personally, I feel that God can do whatever He wants, including sending us dreams, visions, or even visits from our loved ones who've passed. Why some visitations come from "familiar strangers," others, I'm convinced, *are* who they seem to be. We have no idea what God does or does not allow. Most, if not all of our questions will only be answered when we ourselves pass on. I can live with that.

However one must ask the question.If these wonderful things can happen, if these good things can be real, can't the opposite be just as real?

THE STARS AT NIGHT

TEXAS HAD ALREADY called my brother back. We're a close family, and living nearly thousands of miles away from each other made none of us happy. Back then when you dropped someone at the airport you could walk with them to the entrance plank of the plane. We would stay looking out the big glass windows as the tears flowed. We watched for the "sign" from our loved one, the up and down window shade that said "I love you", and we cried when the plane took off. In other words, we didn't do well apart.

At the time I worked in Vancouver for Hewlett-Packard. After the death of Mr. Packard rumors began to flow like water. One ominous day the biggest rumor came true and thousands of us were laid off or relocated. I opted to be one of the last out the door and this bought me six months time.

In the meantime, my father was part-time pastor of a church in Bingen, Washington and working full time at Sacks Fifth Avenue as the head of maintenance. One particular evening he called the house and almost gleefully told my mother and me he'd been laid off due to downsizing.

"Now we can go back to Texas!" He proclaimed.

What ensued was a flurry of craziness. The house had to be sold, Dad had to go to Texas and find a job that would sustain the family for a while, my boys had to be convinced that moving from their friends and girlfriends would not ruin their lives forever... all the mess and stress that comes with a major move. Though both sons had been born in Texas and lived there when very young, they'd grown up in a little town in Washington. Mom had to give up a job she loved at the seminary. It was a hard move. The only thing that kept us going was that we'd be back with family and the little ones who were growing up without us.

As we packed and threw out box after box we wondered about the "other people." Did they know what we were doing? The house grew silent, and I can genuinely state we had no experiences during the last months in that house. On the day we moved out I went back inside to say "goodbye." Later at a rest stop we found that each one of us had done the same thing. It was and still is our favorite house.

We went back to Texas in July of 1999. Texas in July is usually unbearably hot and to make matters worse the people we were buying the place from weren't out! They told my sweet mother they needed two more weeks.

For reasons I still ponder she told them "yes" leaving us to find spots in the barn, shop and shed for a semi truck trailer's worth of furniture and belongings. We took turns staying with my sister and my brother, animals and all. It was a rocky start and made both of my unhappy sons gloat with "See, we shouldn't have come back" comments. Finally, we took over our little farm.

Now, when Mom told the Lord she'd move back she requested several things. One was acreage for my father; two was a swimming pool for my sons and three, a barn for my future horse. God does have a sense of humor because this parcel of property had all three.

After the atmosphere of the "old house" as it's still called, the farm house was very different. None of us felt that strange sense of the place being already occupied. This was a relief and also, I think, kind of a letdown. We'd grown accustomed to having a home with attitude. On the other hand, I was glad nothing had followed us from Washington.

One night, however I was in a deep sleep when I awoke to a young man's face over mine. He was very close and screaming "wake up!" I could tell he was yelling and make out the words even though he didn't make a sound. In my mind, I could hear it. Then he was gone. I didn't see him again.

Cody, however, didn't like his room very much and wouldn't sleep with a fan on even though it was hotter in that part of the house. At the time, I accepted that and asked no questions. It wasn't until much later that I realized why he didn't want the fan on. As anyone interested in the study of ghosts knows, a fan makes a wonderful conduit for "white noise." Cody heard too much when the fan was on.

Once he was awakened by someone pulling his hair. Thinking a neighbor friend of his and Michael's had come to stay all night (soon we had a house full of kids again) and was playing a joke on him, Cody sat up and looked around.

"I know you're here. Very funny." He turned on the light but no one was there.

Though this happened on several occasions Cody took them in stride and was more annoyed than any-thing. We'd lived with much worse. He and I would watch an ever increasing line up of paranormal televi-sion and shake our heads. We'd experienced first-hand most of what these groups were documenting. Some ghost hunters seemed afraid at times and my son and I would look on in disdain. No reason to be afraid, we'd agree. It took a few more years for me to realize how wrong I'd been.

DREAMS AND REALLY LONG DISTANCE PHONE CALLS

IT WAS AROUND this time that we lost my grandmother, "Mamga." The daughter of a Scottish immigrant farmer, she had always lived in the same town most of her life. She had lived long enough to meet her great grandchildren and my sons were fortunate to have known her well into their teenage years. Her loss devastated us all but none more than her older sister, my aunt Gladys. The two sisters lived across the driveway from each other, and our children had spent many happy times running back and forth between the houses.

Some weeks after my grandmother's death, my aunt told me she heard my grandmother's voice saying "Sis?" now and then. Giggy, as we called her, always turned around in surprise but she never saw anything. Still, she felt her sister was close by at times.

Her husband, Alva, (from the sailor and the fire) had passed years before of cancer. Unfortunately, Giggy and Alva were not on good terms the last year of his life. Later, when we learned how sick he was and how quickly the cancer took him, well, it was a very bitter pill for us all. My aunt was full of terrible guilt and regret. At his casket she told me, "No one will love me like Alva Taylor did." Still, her guilt made her give "reasons" as to why their marriage had taken such a bad turn. We loved them both and had not very secretly thought Giggy was wrong. Every visit with her now was full of "why I did that." It was very hard to handle.

On one such visit back to Illinois Giggy told me (before she herself was diagnosed with cancer) that all her bad feelings about Alva were truly gone. Amazed and relieved, I asked her how this change had occurred.

She told me she'd had a dream and in it, she and Alva were walking on beautiful green grass together. Alva, she continued, was leading a horse as they walked. Knowing how Alva had loved his horses and had influenced Dad and we three kids to love horses, too, I took joy knowing that horses were part of his eternity.

I asked her what they talked about and she laughed softly.

"Kid, I couldn't tell you. But I know we laughed, and it's all okay now."

Our visits with her were good again. It's never too late to thank God for peace, here or there, it seems!

It was around then that my dreams began. In my first dream visit with my grandmother we were flying over her old house. I don't' mean in an airplane; we were flying easily and smoothly together. It seemed so natural in my dream.

She had never wanted to sell this particular house anyway but had to in order to buy the house across from my aunt. Suddenly, my grandmother laughed softly and said, "All that fuss about a house!" I noted how radiant and smooth her skin was and how her hair was black again. She was undeniably my grandmother, but she was my *perfect* grandmother. The dream ended too soon but it brought me comfort and to my family as well when I told them.

My second experience wasn't in a dream. My family and I were in Illinois during Memorial Day and as is our custom. We were placing flowers on our loved one's graves. As I walked toward Mamga's grave I silently thought, "Hi, Mamga."

Nothing prepared me to hear back, "Hello" but I did. I'll readily admit it startled me, but what floored me was her tone of voice. It sounded as though perhaps she was upset with me. This bothered me greatly, but I didn't tell anyone about it until I had my third and last dream.

We'd been finding birthday cards in her house made out to her family ahead of time. She'd stopped at May, so there were no cards for me, a July birthday. I recall saying out loud I wished I had one more card from her.

In my third dream, I saw Mamga with a list in her hand. She didn't say a word but smiled and pointed to something on the list. I looked at where she pointed and there was my name and birthday written down. She smiled again and was gone. That was the last time I dreamed of her.

It puzzled me at first as to why she hadn't spoken to me in the third dream, but I remembered my reaction to the voice in the cemetery. The voice sounded "put out" with me or disappointed. I believe my grandmother knew that, and that's why she didn't speak in my third dream. Either I misunderstood the tone of the voice, or it wasn't my grandmother at all. Either way she loved me and clearly didn't want me to be upset. I miss her every day. Meanwhile I wasn't the only family member having strange occurrences.

My brother Edwin was paying bills one day at home. He heard the phone ring but was engrossed in his checkbook and decided to let the machine pick it up. After the beep he heard a familiar voice say, "Hello?" He rose out of his chair to answer the phone. It was then he knew the voice belonged to our grandmother, and that this call was supposedly impossible. He knew the inflection of her voice; how she *said* "hello." Startled he checked the answering machine. No message or voice was recorded, and no number showed on the phone log.

A trick either of the mind or something else? It didn't really matter. My brother was comforted and knew that if Mamga could call, she would. He is as sure as he ever that our grandmother is in Heaven.

Years before our grandmother's death our step-grandfather (nicknamed "Carne") had said before he passed on that he didn't mind going so much if he could only call home once in a while! My brother got that phone call, just not from him. But he did get something even better.

VISITATIONS; SOME WELCOME, SOME NOT SO MUCH

CARNE WAS MAMGA'S husband and the only grandfather we three knew. Our paternal blood grandfather had been killed when our own father was only twelve years old. We never got to know him, but Carne spoiled and loved us as well as any grandfather. He and my brother, Edwin, were especially close.

A chain smoker, he died at home of lung cancer when we were 9, 7 and 2 years of age. He'd been sick for months and sometimes delirious. But two weeks before his death he began to speak clearly and was completely aware of what was happening. One day he awoke from a deep sleep and told my grandmother he'd been to Heaven. With urgency in his voice he told her, "Ask me anything you want to know, and I can tell you for a while." She was afraid to ask! He told of people he'd seen and even his little dog. "And that dog can climb trees now!" He laughingly told her. Days later he told her an angel was outside his window and she should look. Humoring him, I'm sure, she went to the window and heard a "swoosh" sound. She didn't see anything, but she swore by what she heard.

At times Carne would look up in the corner of the ceiling and say, "There they are, but they're a long way yet."

Once he saw some sort of train. Some days later he lapsed into a deep sleep and passed on.

My brother was torn apart from losing Carne. After the funeral he began to have night terrors. I remember how terrified he was, how he didn't seem to know us. It was hard on all of us.

One morning Edwin told us he had a dream.

He told us Carne had walked out of his bedroom closet and sat on the bed next to him. He told my brother that everything would be all right and that Edwin would be with him some day. When Edwin asked, "When?" Carne told him, "Soon." Then he told my brother, "Don't tell anyone because they won't believe you. Not even Sue." (Sue was what our grand-father called me.)

We sat there in stunned silence. We did believe Edwin despite Carne's warning. and the night terrors stopped.

Five years later Edwin had an accident that nearly took his life. The doctors gave him little hope of living, and he was in the hospital for weeks. He made a full recovery but we wondered. Was this what our grandfather meant by "soon?" Edwin had been close to death. Did something change to spare him this time? Or is time itself different in the next life? Guess we'll have to wait and see about that.

Are dream visitations different from apparition sightings? I personally feel that dreams are indeed different than seeing a ghost, and I believe visitations are different than hauntings but we'll explore that in more detail further on.

Six years after Mamga's death, Giggy began to lose her fight with cancer. At age ninety-five she'd fought a long while and had outlived her four siblings and most of her friends. My parents drove to Illinois and brought her home to Texas to live with them for the time she had left. She passed about two months later, in the house, surrounded by all of us. We sang and talked about the past. She slipped away quietly with her family holding her hands and rubbing her feet. Everyone should be so fortunate when facing eternity. We were so glad to do this last thing for her.

I tell you this not to tell you a story about Giggy returning. She didn't. We laugh and say that she kicked the dust off of Texas and never looked back! The point is she died in my parents' house, and we've never had even a hint of her presence. Someone dying in a house does not guarantee a haunting.

We'd joined a church in our town, and my sister-in-law and I decided to attend a party with our Sunday school group. The people hosting the party were funny, down to earth people, but I didn't know them well then.

Their house was outside of town and looked to be an old farm house they'd restored. Lesa and I walked into the charming country kitchen, and I felt that old familiar oddness some places have. Before I even thought I looked at her and said, "This house is haunted." Truly, I wasn't sure I wanted to go inside and told Lesa so.

Our host heard me, and I could have died of embarrassment. I hadn't meant to comment out loud. He held a finger up to his mouth and motioned us over away from the party. I could have died on the spot. Instead of having to explain myself though, he told us his story.

Soon after he and his family had moved in, he was sitting in the living room reading his paper. Suddenly a little boy walked from the kitchen, into the living room and through the wall. Our friend described the little boy in detail. The boy hadn't seemed aware of his presence and didn't make a sound. Since that first time, they'd seen the boy a few more times but he never made a sound, kept to the same path and disappeared. A "ghost" or residual haunting? A pattern simply "recorded" on the fabric of time? I believed my friends, and I suspect what they had was indeed a residual haunting. What's the difference between a residual haunting and some other type of haunting? There's a huge difference between the two and we'll get into that more later.

I'd taken a job in an electric company in town. One lovely fall day I decided to read during my lunch hour. I took my lunch out to my truck parked in the parking lot. Now, I'm an avid reader, and once immersed in a book nothing short of a bomb can get my attention. I was totally relaxed and at ease when I heard a little girls voice outside my open truck window.

"Hello?"

I turned my head fully expecting to see a little girl outside of my window. I shivered and noticed that the hair on my arms and neck stood up. There was no one there and the voice did not repeat. I've since read somewhere that the shiver or the hairs rising sensation happens maybe a second *before* a person sees or hears something paranormal. This is a belief I've since subscribed to. As a matter of fact, if I doubt what I'm experiencing is my imagination or not, I can always check my arms! No hair, not there. This works for me.

The parking lot of an electric company in full day light sure doesn't seem to be the kind of place to hear or see a ghost. But I swear it happened. In my ghost hunting days I fully intended to ask permission to investigate the building and property but I never did. It might have proved very interesting.

A few years after the incident in the parking lot, the electric company lost a dear man. He'd had some health issues but when he died in his sleep one night we were shocked just the same. He was well known in the community and was Fire Chief of the small town a few miles from us. We all dreaded saying goodbye to our friend.

My husband (I had remarried at this point in time) and I arrived at the funeral home for visitation the day before his funeral. Many people were gathered to honor this man, and we had to wait a bit before actually going into the chapel. At one point I opened the doors to see if the crowd had thinned yet. Immediately I saw a large portrait of our friend, in his uniform and smiling. I remember turning to Tom and telling him I had thought they might place such a photo near the casket.

When our turn came to go in, we proceeded quietly down the aisle. Tom turned to me and asked where the portrait was. To my dismay, there *was* no portrait on either side of the casket or anywhere in the chapel. As we approached the casket, we saw he had been dressed in his uniform with his overcoat in his arms. But I had seen him with his uniform on, coat and all. Had I glimpsed our friend or did I simply imagine the portrait?

I work with a dear friend who told me this story second hand from the people who bought his childhood home. Since his telling I've read about more situations just like this.

The house was a big, two story house with a porch all the way across the front of the second story. It was a lovely house with big trees and a huge green lawn. It was also one of the oldest houses in this little town. For a time it was for sale and I would have dearly loved to purchase it but that wasn't to be.

The buyers had begun to renovate the house, tearing down walls and removing wall paper, all that goes with restoring an old home. When a kitchen wall came down, they discovered some small ladies boots. They looked to be made around the early 1900's at least with high tops and laces that were now worn and nearly rotten. Intrigued they set the boots aside and continued their work.

That night the husband awoke in the middle of the night. He decided to go downstairs for a drink and as he passed the porch he looked outside. Standing on the upper porch and looking across the lawn was the very vivid image of a young lady dressed in white, with long blonde hair and a blue sash. Just as quickly she was gone. He swore by what he saw and continued to see the back of this young lady several more times. She never spoke or turned around.

I don't know if someone shared the boots theory with him or if he already knew, but in earlier days people would put items into their walls for good luck. In any case, the family decided to put the boots back inside the wall. The young lady was never seen again but a portrait was painted based on what the owner saw. It shows a young blonde lady, back turned, dressed in white, standing on the upper porch looking out at the yard. It's an amazing portrait.

Why am I sharing these experiences? Friends have been had unexplainable things happen as well. Never think I don't believe what people tell me when they share these kinds of stories. From old, scary buildings and houses to parking lots; full daytime or way past midnight, I've seen or heard it.

THE ARLINGTON HOUSE

Tom was funny and handsome, and he listened to me without "that look" when I talked to him about my interest in ghosts. When we married, Tom and I lived in a little house in Arlington, Texas. I'd been to the house many times before, and it "felt fine" most of the time with one exception.

The hallway leading from the living area to the bedrooms and the guest bathroom made me very uneasy. Until now I hadn't mentioned that to Tom, after all, it had been his house before we married. But when the house became my home too I had to tell him that I always hurried through the hall, and that it seemed darker than the rest of the house. His mouth had dropped open, and that he felt the same thing. He hadn't wanted to make me uneasy and so he didn't tell me. After all, it could have been his imagination.

Once during the night he'd awakened and decided to get a drink. Ignoring the notion of turning the light on, he headed down the hall. Halfway through he said he saw a "white, smoky shape", and before he could react it passed through him. He was unnerved to say the least. So, we shared a fear of the hallway, it seemed. (Note: the white, smoky figures do not seem to be the same as the "white fades.") Whether color, white or gray or even black makes a difference I'm not sure and can't prove. But I suspect it does.

I've always been a restless sleeper and awaken often. At times when this happened my eyes were drawn to the doorway of our bedroom. Nothing was ever there, but I always expected to see someone. When I mentioned that to Tom, he sheepishly said he'd felt the same thing. Whatever it was stayed in the hallway and didn't enter our room.

During one such restless night I'd given up and moved to a comfortable chair in the living room. I fell asleep fairly quickly but began to dream terrible things. Some unseen "things" were chasing me, flying around my head, attacking me. Whatever "they" were, harming me was their intent, I knew. In my dream, I was near a lovely stream, but I was being kept away from it by these creatures for some reason.

Suddenly, a huge man appeared and began to lash out at these things with a sword. I mean a big sword. The things cried out and disappeared as the man cut them down, one after another.

I was aware of sitting in the chair, and that the man was standing in front of me, his back to me, facing outwards toward the dark living room. I could see his feet and that he was wearing brown sandals. I could also see his muscled bare legs and the hem of his white garment. He was very, very tall. The sword he held, I could tell, in both hands and the tip of the blade rested downward on the floor. Amazed is the closest word I can use to what I felt. I was awake.

I felt no fear, only peace and the assuredness that my protector would not leave. In a moment I fell asleep and stayed so until morning.

When I awoke, of course, the man, the angel, was gone. I've not seen him since but I have felt his presence many times. One day, on this side or the other, I hope to meet him face to face.

Tom previously had a dog he loved very much. Unfortunately, his dog got sick and was diagnosed with cancer. Tom had tried every medicine the vet recommended to buy his friend more time but in the end, his dog had to be put down. That pups' picture is on Tom's dresser today.

One night I was gently awakened by pressure on my side of the bed. It felt so much like a dog's paw that my first thought was, *how'd a dog get in?* Turning on the light, no dog or anything else was there. Of course we had to wonder which dog was checking on us.

Sometime later I was recuperating after surgery and was snoozing on the sofa in the living room. It was the middle of the day, and I had just dozed off. Suddenly I felt a gentle pressure on the sofa by my head as though a cat was up on its' legs looking at me. Of course there was no cat. Both times I felt certain the pressure was caused by animal. For as long as I've been alive our family has had cats and dogs. The feeling was very familiar and not one bit scary.

Perhaps they, being spiritually innocent like little children, have the privilege of being able to check on us at times.

PARKER COUNTY
PARANORMAL

LOOK AT US,
WE'RE GHOST BUSTERS!

LOOKING BACK NOW, I'm amazed how naïve we were.

Reading all the books and watching all the programs should have made us more aware. We were eager to be "ghost hunters." I doubt any further warnings at that time would have stopped us from forming Parker County Paranormal. To our credit I really did feel sorry for people who had paranormal experiences and didn't know what to do. Who would they share their stories with? Would people laugh or call them crazy? Each of us on our team had experienced something unexplainable. We were lucky to have a family that listened with open hearts and minds. They believed us; we believed each other. Not everyone is so fortunate, and we knew that. Maybe, we thought, we really could help.

Thanks to technology and web sites, purchasing ghost hunting equipment was easy. We brought a couple of EMF meters, which measure fluctuations in the electromagnetic field. Theory suggest that spirits can manipulate these fields. The meter is used to detect the source of the fluctuations in order to document or promote communication with the other side. We also bought a motion detector, two personal digital recorders, a dual-function thermometer (to measure cold spots, or compare room temperature between the room/ area and a possible cold spot), several flashlights, a stationary voice recorder, a digital camera, a 35 mm camera, and a K2 meter. A K2 Meter detects spikes in electromagnetic energy. Spikes are indicated by the colored lights at the top of the meter. When my future daughter-in-law joined us, she brought four walkie-talkies. We read the directions and figured out how to make these things work. We were open for business!

Our first case was in the apartment of one of our own. My young friend and future team member told us about some strange happenings in her apartment. Her roommate had also experienced some odd happenings. They also claimed to see a little boy at times, peering out of a dark corner of a bedroom. At other times they felt a dark, not so nice presence, usually in one of the bathrooms. It had gotten so bad the girls had started sleeping in one bedroom with the lights on. I remember feeling it just wasn't right to feel so uneasy in your own home.

My brother, Edwin, a fearless and staunch Christian man joined Tom and me on this particular evening. Cross in hand, he crossed the threshold ready to evict whatever was bothering these young girls. Tom began to move around and take pictures while talking with one of the girls about hot spots. I quietly walked around and tried to get a feel of the place. Walking into one bedroom, I stopped and looked into one corner. My friend told me that was where the young boy came from. The place did indeed have that old familiar feeling, though the apartment building was fairly new. More and more we found that age and history of a place didn't necessarily contribute, but older buildings do seem to have a history one can almost touch.

I felt the "boy" there but something else as well. When I mentioned that maybe the boy wasn't the only one, the roommate spoke up. She had seen a "dark shadow man," and he usually could be found in her bathroom. My brother and I exchanged glances. We'd both felt something that didn't seem like a child. At that time, we thought the apartment housed two spirits, one child and one something not so nice. Years later, my mind revisited that thought. Were two spirits really there in that apartment? Or was one spirit posing as a child at times and showing it's true self at other times? At the time we assumed we had two spirits.

I did my usual sit on the floor of each closet and the bathroom and talked out loud to whatever was there. At one point, our friend said the little boy was behind me. I remember my hair standing on end; a sure sign of something paranormal near. It was with pity and gentleness that we prayed for the boy. I then him to look for a light and when he saw it, to run into it as fast as he could.

My brother on the other hand prayed boldly and told whatever dark thing was there to "leave in Jesus name" and to never come back. We said the Lord's Prayer.

The girls said they felt much better, and we smugly packed our things. Feeling somewhat like amateur exorcists, we got into the car and left.

Halfway home our friend called and said they'd heard noises in the kitchen. At this point I was certain the girls were making themselves scared. She wanted us to come back. After a quick discussion with my husband and brother we decided the girls had to take their place back. We told them to pray together and tell whatever it was to leave in Jesus name if they truly thought it was back. Then they were to ignore it. We were firm about that and both girls said they would.

We held our breath all the way home. It was a long drive back, and it was 2 a.m. They didn't call back, and we congratulated ourselves on a first job well done. We were pretty darn proud of ourselves and ready for more action.

Our second case was requested by a good friend of my mother. Her family had built a new house on some property with a very interesting history. The area they lived in (and still do) was the sight of early settlers. She told us that the first young lady to be killed by Indians lived just down the road. At least that was the story.

She told us that shortly after moving into the house, the family began to hear "old" music, and at times they heard people singing hymns. Apparently as soon as someone noticed, it would stop. The grandchildren's play room was always cold no matter the season, and battery toys would go off by themselves. We knew all about that!

One evening our friend was holding her granddaughter watching TV. The upstairs was built on two sides of the house with a "balcony" connecting the sides and looking down on the living room. The balcony looked down on the living room. Her four-year-old granddaughter looked up, pointed and said, "lady and baby." As my friend looked to where the child was pointing up on the balcony and she caught a very quick glimpse of a woman in blue holding something. That was the first actual sighting.

One night my friend awoke to see the lady in blue standing beside her bed. She described her blue dress and bonnet. She said the lady didn't speak and simply disappeared.

As is most always the case, there was another presence in the house. A man made himself known. This man did not seem to be so ambivalent nor as clearly seen. He was dressed in black and had a hat but his features were not clear. He'd been seen in her bedroom and the hallway between that room and the kid's playroom. The feeling she got from him was not a good one.

Other family members had seen items moved or had found lost things in different, nonsensical places. Another familiar pattern we'd experienced as well. Our group was wild with curiosity.

This time our group consisted of Tom and me, my son, Michael, and our young friend and her boyfriend.

Since the apartment investigation our young lady was intrigued and became an enthusiastic member of Parker County Paranormal. Michael turned out to be an awesome video man and we turned him loose at the house to film wherever he "felt" was promising. All of the family was absent except for Mom's friend. As we always did, we began with prayer for our safety and that of our host family. We prayed that whatever dwelt there unseen would move on. After that we always introduced ourselves to those we couldn't see. Two of us sat with Mom's friend for a while, talking softly. The other two and Michael took meters and cameras room to room. We began to hear noises from upstairs, but as soon as a team would advance the noises would stop and then resume on the other side of the second floor. We heard footsteps, popping, and unspecified thuds. This was frustrating for us and our client.

The children's playroom was indeed several degrees colder than the rest of the house, and we checked the vents and the door that led outside for air leaks. Everything seemed tight and we could find no answer for this. Turning out the lights our crew tried in vain to capture something on the K2 meter.

Later, as we reviewed we found nothing on the video or the audio. Our friend was more upset than we were and told us that in the moments after we left her house the noises increased. We tried to reassure her that we believed her. As it turned out, this came to be somewhat of a pattern. At the time, it seemed curious. If a spirit appeared at times, moved things and sang why would that same spirit not manifest and try to make contact with us? Because we were strangers? Maybe, but even then something didn't seem to make sense to me.

We left that night with no answers for our friend or ourselves. I did have a dream later that night where I saw a young girl in blue with two braids in her brown hair. I caught the name "Maggie" and made a note to ask my mother's friend if she knew anyone with that name. When I did remember to ask our friend she turned a bit pale and told me that the name of the girl supposedly killed by Indians was named Maggie. However interesting, it might have been the dream and the information didn't truly help. By the way, Maggie as it turns out was killed by a rattlesnake, not Indians.

Meanwhile I received a phone call from a business in Weatherford. We exchanged emails a few times and finally made a date for the group to come after close one night. We truly felt we were now on our way to becoming a real ghost hunting organization. At this point I even ordered black T-shirts for each member with Parker County Paranormal emblazoned across the front.

The town square of Weatherford is one of those places of yesteryear. The courthouse is very ornate and as busy as always. Surrounding the courthouse are business's of all sorts; cafes, antique shops, the newspaper, and various other shops. It's charming, and I personally love it there. *Parker County Today* magazine called one of these lovely, old buildings home and we were very excited to check out the stories employees told us.

In speaking with our contact we learned that other places around the square had experienced some of the same things. One such place had already been investigated by another Texas paranormal group and they'd had interesting results. Apparently the group had captured EVPs (Electronic Voice Phenomenon) on their recorders. According to our contact, names were heard and verified as belonging to some previous owners of that building. Now we were excited!

Parker County Today was located nearly across the street from a café. We were told that the sounds of keyboards being used and footsteps long after business hours had been heard by late night workers. Nothing had been sighted but the sounds and feel of the place was giving everyone there the jitters. Sounded simple enough.

We met one evening after everyone but our hostess had gone home. She asked to follow us and we were glad to have her along. Again we made a general sweep of the building and found out that the adjoining building belonged to this business, too. It was vacant at the time and being renovated, but no one was there yet. We asked if we could have access to that building as well and were told we could. Michael and his video camera climbed the stairs to check it out, and before he had even made it to the top my son knew something here was different.

He told us that this side of the business was "much darker" than the working side. He didn't mean literally although there was no electricity connected. Michael was downright reluctant, he told us, to even enter the second room on the left. But he made himself go in and video. On review we found nothing. Despite his feelings, we decided to make this building a part of our investigation as well.

After our group had divided and separately checked out the working business we left a recording device running. I planned to leave it there all night and asked our host to remove it when she came in the next day. I would then return and pick it up. Everyone left, I pushed "start" on the recorder and softly shut the door.

Again our groups divided. My friend and her fiancée, my future daughter-in-law and Michael went up first. Tom, my brother, and I stayed behind and gleaned more ghost stories from our hostess. It was a lovely night.

When the first group came out, they were very excited. The girls had both heard something strange and taken many pictures. Michael still had nothing on video but he was adamant that there was something wrong up there. Group two and I plus our host climbed the stairs.

The place was fully dark, like I said; with no electricity. The imagination could run away with a person up on that second floor. There was nothing but a small desk/table in the whole place. I felt drawn to the last room on the left and began to ask questions using our K2 meter. Almost at once we got light up responses on the meter! I had never seen anything like it. My questions were answered quickly, and the lights of the meter stayed green until the next question was asked. We could hardly believe it. Our hostess was impressed as well and saw for herself what was happening.

Hardly believing our luck, we took some more pho-tos and recordings. Satisfied we'd covered the place well, we went back downstairs when the K2 didn't respond anymore. We truly felt somehow that it was time to leave. The girls however wanted to go back up again. I wasn't for it and told them so. They went anyway.

The girls weren't upstairs for five minutes when they came back down. One of them told us that they both felt "they weren't wanted there" and that whatever it was wanted them to leave.

We packed up and talked to our new friend for a while, telling her what we would do next with the recordings, video, and photos. We agreed to meet back during business hours in one week. We had a lot of things to review.

Michael Graham, Jon Shuley, Larissa Moore, Tom Driscoll, Ellen Driscoll, Edwin Newton, Cody Graham, Breyanna Davis

Jon is looking up the dark staircase in the Parker County Today magazine building.

Ellen asking for questions and watching for responses from the K2 meter.

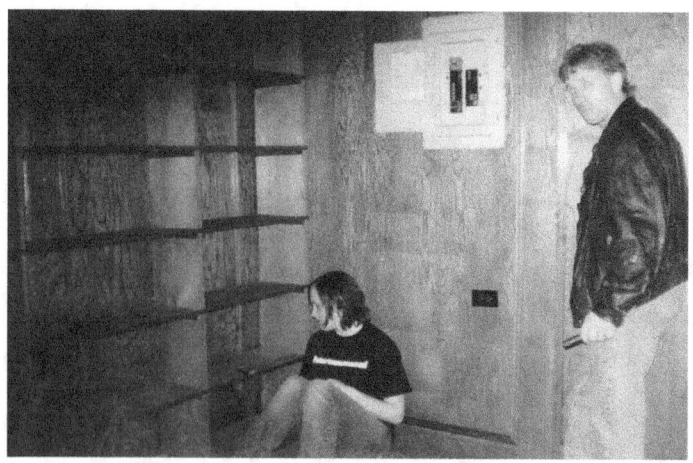

Larissa and Edwin asking questions for the digital recorder.

Amber and Michael investigating the room next to the first one. Varied responses in that room but nothing significant.

Ellen and Larissa. Notice orbs in the room.

Michael alone with photographer.

Tom asks questions while watching the K2 meter.

⇒ PARKER COUNTY ⇐

TODAY

OUR COUNTY'S MAGAZINE

Ghost Stories

The Downtown Cafe.
The Witch's Tomb. The Baker Mansion.
JUST WHAT EXACTLY ARE
THOSE THINGS THAT GO
BUMP IN THE NIGHT?

INSIDE:

KAY GRANGER
talks health care and cutting horses

FAMILY TREES
tips and tricks for progenitor prospectors

www.parkercountytoday.com

0 94922 53668 6

October 2009 • $3.95 USA

VOICES FROM BEYOND

DUE TO MY good ears I was nearly always the one to review audio recordings. I would go to a room by myself with no distractions, put on my headphones, and just listen. The first time I would simply "listen," rewind, and begin again. If I did hear something questionable, I marked the place on the recording for the others to hear. It's easy to drift when reviewing video or audio, so you have to be awake, alert, and patient.

After listening to the first part of the investigation I made notes that our group needed to talk less but other than that, nothing. But during the second half, in the empty part of the building, I caught something. It sounded like a growl. I played it back again and again, marked it, and listened again. It still sounded like a growl. And it gave me the shivers.

I hurried to my Mother's house and put head phones on her ears. My mother, was a very skeptical almost believer and that's just what I wanted. I watched her as she listened and saw her mouth drop. She took the headphones off and looked at me.

"What's it sound like to you, Mom?"

"It's a growl," She said without hesitating. "It sounds like a growl."

I was ecstatic and handed the headphones to my husband. He told me it sounded like "a chair scraping across the floor." I was rather irritated that he didn't hear a growl, but there were no chairs in that part of the building anyway so I accepted what he said. Calling the rest of the group together, most heard a growl or a "growling sound" of some sort. But we all heard it. We were ecstatic and could hardly wait to show our host.

When we arrived for the review there were several more people waiting to see what we had!

We explained we hadn't caught much and absolutely nothing on the business side of the building but... and we played the growl over and over as each person wanted to listen to it. It seemed to all present that whatever it was in the building was not happy with us being there, but the investigation was a success.

We began to get calls from a certain area of town. Rather, this was (and is) an area outside of town, and if I said the name, people in this area would know exactly where I was talking about. For their sake, we'll have to stay anonymous.

The first of these calls came from a woman whose husband was a truck driver. Being on the road so much had her alone most of the time. According to this lady she saw and heard a "cowboy" like figure. At least he wore a western hat and was very tall. She thought some of the noises she'd been hearing sounded like boots on a hard wood floor. This figure wasn't a white, wispy creature; it was very dark, almost black. That description alone made us determined to go and see if we couldn't get this poor lady some comfort. Maybe we could at least figure out some of the noises occurring in her home.

However, the strangest part of her story was that a little, man-like "creature" had been in her house, hiding in the kitchen. In addition, her daughter, who lived next door, had seen the thing trying to get in after our client had locked up that particular door. Her description of the little man matched her mother's exactly. We had interviewed each woman separately. Personally, I had never heard of anything like this and neither had anyone in our group. If we did see the thing, we weren't sure how to deal with it but if we got evidence on video maybe we could find someone who had and would know what to do.

We arrived near dark and toured the house and property. There were two out buildings to check out as well. We decided to check out the house and property simultaneously. Both groups had warlike talkies but decided to keep silent unless we spotted something obvious or someone outside fell into a well or something. It was dark, and there were no street lights.

Our first house group began to check where our client said she'd heard most of the noises except for the boot sounds. It was during this time that our client told us about an old mirror in this same room. She had covered it with a cloth and told us she had seen faces in it.

We took pictures of the mirror but saw nothing in the mirror ourselves. Taking photos of a mirror is a bit of a trick due to the flash and the possibility of the mirror reflecting back. Soon we did indeed begin to hear odd sounds in the room. It didn't take long to figure out there was a family of squirrels living in the attic space over that particular room. Michael went outside and climbed up a ladder and saw evidence of the little creatures burrowing. That explained part of what our client had been hearing. Still, we hadn't heard the sound of boots, so we decided to switch places with our outdoor group and some EVP work. EVPs (EVP stands for Electronic Voice Phenomenon) are sounds or voices picked up by a recording device. These sounds cannot be heard with the human ear to qualify as an EVP. In this case, we gathered in the blackness our clients' living room, and I began to ask questions in hopes that our playback would reveal answers.

After some time recording, we regrouped to talk to our client. No boot noises had been heard, no apparitions had been seen, and our only evidence so far was a family of squirrels. Nothing had been detected in the outbuildings either. Still, we had audio and video to review. We promised to call her in one week with anything we might have found.

Upon review, we heard nothing on audio or video. Personally, I wondered if our client was nervous staying alone in the house so much. It would certainly be understandable. I called her and told her what we hadn't found, but she stuck to her story of the things she'd seen. I've never yet doubted that a client saw or experienced *something* unnatural. In this instance we'd solved only part of the puzzle. The noises from one room came from animals living above. Beyond that, we could neither prove nor disprove what our client told us. We felt badly about not being able to help more. Even a second trip to this house and property didn't give us any evidence. Our group ended up praying with her and giving her permission to call us 24/7 if she was afraid.

Our second call from this same area was a bit different.

This house had been the sight of a suicide of our clients' family member. The sadness weighed heavily on these people yet they were cheerful, wonderful people, who made us very welcome. The suicide had occurred a few years previous. They'd heard voices, seen lights, and their doorbell rang when the deceased man's son visited the house. Our group had a solemn chore ahead. We could tell these nice people wanted very much to know that at least one of the voices belonged to their family member. Our hearts went out to them, and we knew we had to be very careful not to simply give them what they wanted most without evidence.

We began by showing up before dark in order to get somewhat familiar with the property. When you're part of the group investigating outside it's nice to know where buildings, fences, and other obstacles are before night sets in. After dividing into two groups, we checked that our walkie-talkies were set to the same channel and proceeded.

The actual house where the suicide took place had been removed and had been replaced with a shop building. The grandfather of the family took us to the exact spot where he had found his son. It seemed you could feel the sadness. We tried audio at that point and video. Afterward we walked the rest of the property and thought we'd found one mysterious light the family had been seeing. A burning "dusk to dawn" light could be seen through the trees. When tree limbs brushed across the view, it seemed the light disappeared. However our clients told us this was not what they were seeing. Strike one.

In the house nothing obvious was detected by audio and video, so we decided to gather in the living room and do an EVP session. As soon as we got everyone seated and quiet we realized we had one huge problem. Someone outside was shooting fireworks! Though we proceeded on with our session it became increasingly clear that we probably wouldn't get much out of our recording.

We said a warm goodbye to our clients and promised to return with whatever results we might have. Instead, Michael pulled me aside. He'd been anxious to get something for these people as we all were and had gone to another room to see if he could hear something from his recordings.

"Listen," he whispered. "What do you hear?"

As I cupped one ear over the headphone of his digital recorder I heard something that sounded like, "Up here." After those words were other garbled words, but I couldn't make them out. Michael had marked where he was when this part of the recording was made. We knew he'd been in the hallway between the bedrooms. Amazed we'd heard anything over the rockets outside, we decided to let our clients listen, one at a time, with the headphones. No one was to say out loud what they heard until everyone had a chance to listen.

Sure enough each person agreed. We all heard "up here" on the digital recording. What they didn't agree on was whose voice it was! As much as they wanted to hear their loved ones voice I had to respect them for wanting to be absolutely sure. One family member thought that the voice was that of a beloved family friend they'd lost not long before. Everyone agreed to hearing two voices on the recording but none could say for certain who the voices were. Our group left and promised to follow up with or without more evidence.

Nothing else was found on either video or audio. Tom and I traveled back to the house. We talked to the son of the suicide victim, and he was comforted that we'd heard something. Whether it was his father or not, he said, he knew his dad wasn't far away, and he was glad. This was one remarkable young man.

After review we had nothing else to report for our clients but again told them to keep us appraised if anything new happened. We left them our promise to answer on a 24/7 basis and hoped we'd brought them some peace.

Around this time when I called the group together I only had to ask, "Guess where our next investigation is?" and they'd answer in unison. We began to wonder if there was any *other* part of our county that was haunted, or if the spirits had all moved in together! One story we heard over and over again was that Satanists had worshipped in that area years ago. Another was that this land was cursed by Native Americans. Another was that some residents (never ones anyone could name) practiced black magic. Whatever the truth was, it did seem odd that most of our calls came from the same nearly rectangular area. To this day we don't know why this area was, and maybe still is, so active.

In any case we met with our new clients at their home after a brief interview with me by phone. These people were very nice, but you could tell they were holding something back. Finally, the couple reluctantly told us that their young grandson had died on their property not very long ago. Our hearts broke for them and not just because of their loss. They dared to hope that the paranormal activity might be the presence of their grandson, though they didn't say so. I think we tried even harder to be very careful with these cases. It was too easy to sympathize and unknowingly give the family what they wanted. That wouldn't be fair or right in any way no matter our empathy.

They told us they heard giggling and that their little dog would react to things they could not see. Items in the house would be moved at times and later found in unusual places. At night, our client's wife would be awakened by hearing her name from the other end of the house. Checking, neither she nor her husband found anything. Lights were turned off and on frequently; it was nearly a text book case. She also said one of the bedrooms was colder than other rooms. We decided to begin there.

After dividing up as usual we took video of the room as well as digital photos. We snapped some 35mm photos as well and usually took pictures with both cameras when one room or area seemed to be most active (according to our clients). We did get immediate "orb" results but nothing that might not be dust motes. Orbs are balls of light that many regard as spirits but are often nothing more than bugs or dust. Hardly ever did we take orbs into much account. It's just too easy for an orb to be something else.

After a time with both groups taking K2 readings and doing work with digital video, we decided to gather in the living room with our clients and do an EVP session. We asked a few questions, pausing in between for answers. The K2 seemed to light up twice in answer to our questions, and we were very anxious to review our audio.

After saying goodbye to our clients we prayed and promised we'd be in touch whether we found evidence or not. They were very nice, sad people, and we hoped we could help.

Reviewing later that next night, I heard something on our digital recorder. The voice was very clear and distinct. I heard what sounded like a young child say "pink!" in kind of an excited tone. If I had to guess, the voice sounded more like a little girl. This was very exciting. Tom heard the same thing I did and as excited as we were, I wanted more verification. That next day, I took the recording to work, not telling my co-workers what they were listening for.

Of the five people I asked to listen, two women did not hear anything! Even when we removed the headphones and played just the recorder, those same two could not hear the word, "pink" or any word at all. Another person in the room could not believe it and said, "I can hear it across the room-how can you not?"

I called a team member who had the same device running at the same time and much to my surprise, her recorder had *nothing* on it. No little child's voice; nothing. I've since learned that this occurs at times whereby two digital recorders, recording at the same time, may not pick up on the same sounds. At this time, that was news to me.

This recording was still a success in our book, but we didn't understand why the voice would say, "pink" like it did. What did that mean, if anything? Then it occurred to a team member. She always wore pink socks on our investigations for good luck. She'd been sitting cross-legged on the floor during our EVP session. Her jeans must have pulled up enough for her pink socks to be seen.

Our clients heard the voice when we went to their house and played it for them, but neither could truly identify the voice. It seemed like a child's voice to all of us, but it was not readily familiar to the couple. In a way, I think they were relieved. It would be a hard thing indeed to know your grandchild was not at rest and perhaps wandering around your home. We said fond goodbyes, and I hope these wonderful people have some peace in their lives.

I got a phone call one day from a different town. That was a welcome change for certain! But as this woman began to speak to me, I had to wonder. Her boyfriend had committed suicide, and her son had seen the man open the patio doors and come into the house. She asked me what my group would do, and I told her we would pray and then try to ask the spirit to move on. Immediately her tone changed and she told me she'd "have to think about it." We hung up but I was shocked. Had the woman wanted her late boyfriend to stay with her and not move on? That's the way it seemed to me. The terrible decision she seemed to have made haunted me for quite a while.

Another call (yes, from our usual area) told me of another suicide. This woman's brother had hung himself from a tree in her yard. I can only imagine the grief and horror of such a thing. And of the regret the victim might have felt when they realized this act was forever. Lots of intense emotion.

We met the family near dark as always and walked the property. Our clients mostly wanted their loved one to know that they loved them still and that they were all right. My heart broke for this sister as she told me that once while driving home she had seen her brother walking on the side of the road and had waved at him, realizing a second later how impossible that was. She jerked her truck around but saw nothing. Again, was it wishful thinking or had she truly seen her brother?

We had a problem in this case, and it wasn't fireworks. Before any investigation we would gently urge our clients to keep the children away and to keep family members and friends at a minimum. However, we had a few young ones around, and they were very curious! Despite our attempts at investigating, we didn't get much audio that wasn't damaged by background talk and noise. I would have like to have returned, but we never got the chance. It's very frustrating for the team and the client when time is wasted. Video yielded nothing. Unfortunately we hadn't been able to help at all.

One investigation almost didn't happen. Our lady client had a son who did not believe in ghosts or ghost hunters. She told us we'd have to schedule a time when her son wasn't home. She believed a ghost of a little girl was attached to her. She had no idea of who the girl might be. but she had also seen the figure of a man she thought to be her father. We agreed on a time and called the group together.

After splitting up into two groups we proceeded to walk the house and property. Michael kept saying he "felt nothing" but we knew this wasn't necessarily a prerequisite for a haunting. Still it did seem that this place seemed very ordinary with none of the "hair static" or cold spots we sometimes felt.

Some time into the investigation our client told us the girl was standing behind her, clinging to her skirts. We saw nothing but did take video, photos and audio. We prayed that the little girl and any other spirits might leave and go "into the light." Our client told us that it "didn't work" and that the little girl wouldn't leave her.

We never got a glimpse of the man figure, and she said he wasn't there. I began to wonder why *we* were there. Our client seemed almost determined that "her spirits" did not want to leave. Perhaps she wanted us there to verify something for her. We were never sure. Our group left, and I felt terrible that a little girl was "lost" and clinging to a life she no longer belonged to. Not for the first time I pondered why God would leave a little child behind. Why didn't an angel come for them at their time of death? Who was this little girl anyway?

Most of our investigations were similar in that we didn't "catch" much on audio or video. The growl we caught and the "pink" recording were the most remarkable events we had. The phone calls to Parker County Paranormal began to peter off except for the crank calls we received about once a week.

I began to question almost everything to do with ghost hunting. At first I figured it was partly disappointment that the drama of television ghost hunting didn't apply to us. But that wasn't all of it, I knew. When we began, I truly thought my gift of sensitivity could help others; maybe even free spirits who couldn't leave this plane for some reason. I knew my heart motive was right, and I loved the paranormal. It was a perfect match. Wasn't it?

THE TRUTH

Two years into Parker County Paranormal I began to notice how far I was slipping into the dark.

If any kind of paranormal TV show was on, that's what I watched. Re-runs or new, I watched and re-watched each and every episode of every program. Every book I bought or asked for was based on ghosts or the dark side of the paranormal experience. I lived for any program that involved spirits and ghost hunting. More than that, my viewing turned from a passion to learn into simply an obsession with ghosts.

Deep down a part of me knew something was very different, but I tried hard to ignore that small voice. I found myself praying less about what my motive was as an investigator. My heart, if you will, began to feel uneasy, and my mind resented it and fought against it. This was who I was, who I'd always been. I knew it, my family knew it, and my friends knew it. What was the big deal anyway? I got angry at anyone whose total support I questioned.

My sister-in-law's mother came for a visit from Oregon, and I found myself explaining why I was investigating. She hadn't asked. She expressed her concern that I was doing the right thing, but I'd brought it up. Something was, if you will, haunting me.

Truth be told, I was no longer certain that what I was doing was in God's will for me. I'd pulled the groups advertisement and prayed no one would call me. In other words, I'd begun to make a 180 turn and was trying to keep it from myself. That's when I heard the words that changed everything.

"Old friend, I don't think you're supposed to confront anymore. Let the angels do that."

I stared at the screen for minutes. That was it. I wouldn't have been the least surprised to hear a loud "click" in my mind. Absolute assuredness came over me. I searched my mind and soul for a mistaken message. There was no doubt and no mistake.

Have you ever had a question answered so completely that you couldn't begin to deny it, even when you tried? A certainty so revealed to you that there was no way to deny it?

Few things in my life have been absolutely sure with no doubts or second guesses. This was one of those. I may be over-emphasizing this point a bit! I cannot possibly convey to someone who doesn't know me what this meant. It felt as though a relationship I'd always counted on was irrevocably over. No words or actions could put it together again. The door was slammed and locked against me. I didn't know what to feel, really. Relief wasn't what I felt and neither was regret. Just certainty that this was what God wanted me to do for my own sake and for my best life path. It was over.

I did have one question, however. What was I supposed to do now?

For a few weeks, I just let this all sink in. I didn't do anything and at first, I didn't even talk about it with my friends and family. As I stated before I had to talk to my husband about what had happened, and he too was dismayed. We had this love of the paranormal in common! Our group, though inactive of late, was our baby together. He didn't know what to say to me. But he respected my resolve and my certainty. He knew that for me to give up something that had always been such a part of me was serious. I believe he'd been less surprised if I'd told him I was becoming a vegetarian. (Knowing how I love a good steak.) But he backed me up and didn't even try to question me about this change. When one of my former favorite programs came on that next week, he simply changed the channel without comment.

What I watched and what I read became instantly different to me except for a slip of rebellion when I tried to "test" the issue. I had no real interest in the programs I'd always set my watch by. My searches on Google no longer included visits to paranormal sites. I kept expecting to miss these things. But I didn't. The fact that I didn't filled me with dismay.

After a month or so more, I told my kids, family and friends about this change in my life. I don't think most of them believed me and probably thought (though none admitted it) that I'd either gone off my rocker or had some sort of holy roller religious experience. I'd get over it; I imagine some of them thought. True as that was, I didn't know what to do with me either.

I began to earnestly pray about how to fill this gap in my life. There had to be something to do with this interest that was so much a part of me and yet keep in tune with my new mindset. I began to read books that dealt with the *other* side of the paranormal; accounts of angels and heavenly intervention. Although such had always been a part of my interest in the supernatural, I'd nearly abandoned the search for the paranormal as it related to the greatest supernatural being of all, God.

According to the Bible, we are surrounded by spiritual warfare as is spoken of in Ephesians 6:12 "For our struggle is not against flesh and blood, but against the rulers, against the authorities, against the powers of this dark world and against the spiritual forces of evil in the heavenly realms" (NIV).

Of course I'd heard of spiritual warfare most of my life. I was raised in church, saved at age fifteen and duly baptized, my father is a Baptist minister; I'd heard of it. But I hadn't realized that what was happening to me at this time in my life was this; I was in the middle of my own personal spiritual battle.

WHAT AM I SUPPOSED
TO DO NOW?

AND NOW COMES the part of my story that I've almost dreaded.

At this point what I've shared has been part of my past. How do you put that "close to the veil," sensitive part of you to rest?

You don't.

What you start doing with that special, spiritual side of yourself is to re-direct it. God made us, and He doesn't mess up. We do, He doesn't. So, if He made us, we can't help but dabble in the paranormal, can we? Well...

First you must remember that the paranormal, the supernatural is easily defined and described. Per *Merriam-Webster's* definition "Paranormal" is "impossible to explain scientifically or understood in terms of science," and synonyms are "supernatural," "unnatural" or "prenatural."

Notice that the supernatural or the paranormal does not only apply to the dark world of ghosts, spirits, goblins, demons, whatever. Seems to me that the greatest supernatural entity of all is God himself. So let's start there.

According to the Bible, (New International Version) God made the earth. Genesis is believed to be written by Noah. "In the beginning, God created the Heaven's and the Earth."

Pretty hard to fathom that before God spoke this existence into tangible fact, there was nothing.

So studying, learning, and investigating those things that are "above normal" or more than normal isn't wrong in and of itself. It may seem simple and overstated, but I had to get this straight in my own mind. The world of the supernatural or the paranormal does not have to be the study of only all things dark.

When I was younger I knew this by instinct. Ever hear a child pray? There is no doubt or hesitation in their minds that God hears them. They believe in the supernatural, more than normal power of God.

So, we've confirmed that there's more to our interest in the paranormal than ghost stories.

But what does the Bible say about ghosts?

There are a few references to ghosts, and at least one example of a ghost or spirit coming back to deliver a message. This is where it gets tricky. Jesus himself refers to ghosts twice. It doesn't get any more mysterious than the Bible.

The first reference to a ghost that I can find is in Samuel 1:28 (NIV) in the Old Testament.

To sum up, King Saul had troubles of all kinds.

The Philistines had gathered to fight against Israel. The prophet Samuel was dead and the Bible said "all Israel mourned for him." Meanwhile, King Saul had banished all mediums and spiritists from the land.

When the king catches sight of the Philistine army, he is terrified. He asked the Lord but God had since given up answering the king in dreams or the prophets. God knew Saul wasn't asking for His advice, only for protection and victory. And remember, Saul had driven away the man God (through Samuel) had chosen as king of Israel, David. They were not on good terms, to say the least.

Now Saul decides to get some help from one of the very kinds of people he drove out, a medium. He asks his servant where to find one and he tells his master of a woman who is a medium. Saul disguises himself and goes to her at night. He does not tell her who he is and promises no harm will come to her when she reminds him of the kings' edict. She asks who he wants to her to "bring up" and he tells her Samuel.

As soon as she sees Samuel (or the familiar spirit who appears to be him) she cries out, "Why have you deceived me? You are Saul!"

Now, either she was surprised to see a real spirit because she was a fake or she was given this piece of knowledge from God himself. One thing I hadn't realized until much later is that *she* saw the spirit. Saul did not or he wouldn't have asked her what she saw.

Saul asks her who she sees and she says, "An old man wearing a robe is coming up out of the ground." (Out of the ground? Interesting.) Why would the prophet Samuel, promised of God, come "out of the ground", not down from Heaven? Another question.

The Bible says, "Then Saul knew it was Samuel." The Bible does not say, "Saul knew it was someone who looked like Samuel," nor does it say, "Saul was tricked and thought it was Samuel." Perhaps it *was* Samuel. God can do what He wants and is not limited to our understanding.

Saul bows down and puts his head to the ground.

The spirit of (supposedly Samuel) asks, "Why have you disturbed me by bringing me up?"

We don't know at this point if the medium has fainted dead away, or if she also sees or hears Samuel. We find this in old Testament of First Samuel, chapter 28, beginning in verse 15.

"I am in great distress," Saul says. "The Philistines are fighting against me, and God has turned away from me. He no longer answers me in dreams or through prophets so I have called on you."

"Why do you consult me, now that the Lord has turned from away from you and become your enemy? The Lord has done what He predicted through me. The Lord has torn the kingdom out of your hands and given it to David. Because you did not obey the Lord or carry out His fierce wrath against the Amalekites, the Lord has done this to you. The Lord will hand over both Israel and you to the Philistines and tomorrow you and your sons will be with me."

Saul was filled with fear and fell full length to the ground. The Bible tells us he hadn't eaten all day and had no strength, but the medium gave him food, and his men encouraged him to eat. It was his last meal. The next day he and his sons were dead, and the army of Israel was captured by the Philistines.

We don't know how the spirit of Samuel departed. The Bible doesn't tell us these things. But some things are clear. God allows what He allows. I have no reason to believe this was not Samuel. I've read a lot about these verses, and some people mention the strange words of Samuel "coming out of the ground" as proof that this was not Samuel. I don't know about that, but I know that either it was Samuel's spirit, ghost, or something else altogether, and God allowed this to happen for His own reasons. But what a story about the world of the paranormal!

The second mention of the dead rising, which might be defined as "ghosts" is in Matthew 27:52–53. "The tombs also were opened. And many bodies of the saints who had fallen asleep were raised, and coming out of the tombs after his (Jesus) resurrection they went into the hold city (Jerusalem) and appeared to many."

Now I believe that these people were literally raised from the dead and not ghosts, but I'm betting that some of the people they appeared to *thought* they were ghosts! But this verse states that the "body" of these saints was raised. Ghosts don't have a body, so I don't hold much with this verse proving ghosts exist and interact. Nonetheless, this verse is pretty awesome.

As I said earlier Jesus himself took on the subject of ghosts twice that we know of.

According Matthew, chapter 14, beginning with verse 25, we read that Jesus went up on a mountainside to pray alone. The disciples went fishing and their boat was some distance from shore. They must have gotten tired of waiting on Jesus, we don't know, but they went ahead. Shortly before dawn, Jesus went out to them, walking on the lake. When the disciples saw him walking on the water, they were terrified. "It's a ghost," they said, and cried out in fear. But Jesus immediately said to them, "Take courage! It is I. Don't be afraid."

"Lord, if it's you," Peter replied, "tell me to come to you on the water."

Apparently, Peter wasn't sure he was buying this. Notice he says "If it's you."

"Come." Jesus said.

But when Peter saw the wind, he was afraid and began to sink, crying out, "Lord, save me!"

Immediately Jesus put out his hand and caught him. "You of little faith," he said, "why did you doubt?"

Frankly I always thought Peter got a bit of a raw deal here. I mean, none of the others dared to even try and walk on the water! Still, it surely proves what can be done with faith and what can be undone with doubt.

Note, too, that although Jesus rebukes Peter a bit about doubting, he does not rebuke the men for crying out the "ghost" word. Jesus had no trouble, at other times, in chiding his men for not believing, but he doesn't tease them about their belief in ghosts. Maybe he simply thought there was no point, we don't know.

Sometime after this, and in the same book of Matthew, chapter 17, verses 1-3 (NIV) Jesus took Peter, James, and John his brother and led them up a high mountain. (Why only these three? Perhaps they were the ones that needed confirmation the most?)

The Bible goes on to say, "Jesus was transfigured before them, and his face shone like the sun, and his clothes became white as light. Just then there appeared before them Moses and Elijah, talking with Jesus.

Peter said, "Lord, it is good for us to be here. If you wish, I'll put up three shelters-one for you, one for Moses and one for Elijah."

A bright cloud covered them suddenly and a voice from the cloud said, "This is my son, whom I love. Listen to him!"

When the disciples heard this they were terrified and fell face down on the ground. The sight of Jesus, Moses and Elijah entranced them, I guess but the voice thundering from the cloud was too much. Jesus came and touched them saying, "Get up, don't be afraid." When they looked up, they saw no one but Jesus.

As they came down from the mountain Jesus said, "Don't tell anyone what you have seen until the son of man has been raised from the dead."

One of the disciples asked, "Why do the teachers of the holy law say that Elijah must come first?"

Jesus replied, "I tell you Elijah has already come and they did not recognize him but did everything they wished to him. In the same way, the Son of Man will suffer at their hands."

And then the disciples knew Jesus was talking about John the Baptist.

Okay, some interpret these verses as proof of reincarnation. The men all knew that the scriptures said Elijah had to come back before the Messiah. Jesus as good as said that John the Baptist was the Old Testament prophet, Elijah.

On the other hand, how could John the Baptist be Elijah reincarnated if the men had just seen Elijah with Moses and Jesus? My head began to spin at this point in my reading. This is an ice breaker for any Bible study or any paranormal meeting of the minds.

Did Jesus mean that John was Elijah literally or figuratively? As for me, I'm not sure but this is a great (and true) supernatural story, isn't it? I mean, even if that is not what Jesus meant, he himself (that is his appearance) was *changed*, and he appeared with two Old Testament men long gone. How'd they get there so suddenly? Beat, that for paranormal.

Now the following verses aren't included in any ghost references in the Bible but maybe they should be. If this isn't a tale of the supernatural, I don't know what would be.

On the day Jesus rose from the dead, and after the disciples had found his tomb empty, two of his followers were walking to a village called Emmaus. They were heavy hearted and the Bible says their faces were down cast.

They were walking and talking when jesus himself began to walk alongside them, but they were kept from recognizing him. These verses are in Luke 24:1–33, New International Version, by the way. This verse has been talked about and argued over for years. Why did they not recognize Jesus? They knew him, didn't they? Read on, it gets better:

> He (Jesus) asked, "What are you discussing together as you walk along?"
>
> They stood still, their faces downcast. One of them, names Cleopas, asked him, "Are you the only one visiting Jerusalem who does not know the things that have happened there in these days?"
>
> "What things?" he asked.
>
> "About Jesus of Nazareth," they replied, "He was a prophet, powerful in word and deed before God and all the people. The Chief priests and our rulers handed him over to be sentenced to death, and they crucified him; but we had hoped that he was the one who was going to redeem Israel. And what is more, is the third day since all this took place. Also some of our women amazed us. They went to the tomb early this morning but didn't find his body. They came and told us they had seen angels who said he is alive. Then some of our friends went to the tomb and found it empty, just as the women had said, but they did not see Jesus."
>
> He said to them, "How foolish you are and how slow to believe all the prophets have spoken! Didn't the Messiah have to suffer these things and then enter his glory?" And beginning with Moses and all the prophets, Jesus

explained to them what was said in the scriptures concerning him.

As they came to the village, Jesus continued on as though he was going farther but the two men strongly urged him to stay with them saying, "Stay with us, for it is nearly evening; the day is almost over." So he went inside with them.

When Jesus was at the table with them, he took break, gave thanks, and broke it and began to give it to them. Then their eyes were opened and they recognized him, and he disappeared from their sight.

Note, Jesus didn't get up and leave, no mention of goodbyes and hugs, he simply wasn't there anymore.

The men asked each other "Weren't our hearts burning within us while he talked to us?"

They got up and returned to Jerusalem. There they found the eleven disciples and those others with them, all together.

"It is true!" they said. "The Lord has risen and has appeared to Simon!" And they told of how they recognized Jesus when he broke the bread.

Supernatural, paranormal stuff? Uh, yeah, it sure is! But Jesus wasn't done visiting just yet.

In Luke 24:36, the Bible says, "While they were still talking about this, Jesus himself stood among them and said to them, 'Peace be with you.'"

So, he reappeared from nowhere. If the same two men who'd only recently seen Jesus disappear were still there in the room, they must have been freaked out to see him reappear.

The disciples were startled and frightened and thought they were seeing a ghost.

He said to them, "Why are you troubled, and why do doubts arise in your minds? Look at my hands and my feet. It is I! Touch me and see; a ghost does not have flesh and bones, as you see I have."

Jesus even ate in front of them to prove his point.

Jesus actually referred to a ghost. Many argue that this means Jesus is verifying the existence of ghosts. Some say that he, knowing their superstitions and beliefs, is simply reassuring them on their level, knowing that they believe in ghosts. Both arguments have merit.

Why didn't Jesus simply rebuke the disciples by saying, "Look, dummies, there are no such things as ghosts!"

But He didn't. Does that prove He believed in ghosts? Does this prove that ghosts exist?

GHOSTS, SPIRITS, DEMONS AND ANGELS

ONE THEORY THAT may be truth is that ghosts, hauntings, spirits are no more than residual hauntings. Residual hauntings, according to Wikipedia, are "repeated playbacks of auditory, visual, olfactory, and other sensory phenomena that are attributed to a traumatic event, life-altering event, or a routine event of a person or place, like an echo or a replay of a videotape of past events." There is no involvement with the living. The playback, if you will, would happen whether anyone saw it or not. I really don't have a problem believing in the possibility of residual hauntings. In fact, some of the older ghost stories I have read nearly always follow that pattern. A ghost is seen or heard; the person witnessing this gets scared and tells others. That's about it.

Also according to Wikipedia,

> "The kind of energy needed that might be involved and how such 'playbacks' are triggered are unknown, rendering the theory currently unprovable. Some proponents of this theory state that a specific state of brainwaves is necessary to experience a playback, while others claim that the 'viewing' person needs some physic ability."

If residual phenomena makes up the majority of what we know as hauntings, this occurrence would be as old as humans themselves. From the beginning mankind has experienced all kinds of drama and routine. Could this be where the whole thing started? When did the first person see the first "ghost" anyway? After he or she had this experience, you know they told someone what they saw. As the population increased, so would death and so would residual hauntings a.k.a. ghost sightings. Stories would be told and passed down for generations, and eventually written down. The first ghost stories?

Could this really be the way it all began? What about interactive hauntings? What of family members coming back (or never leaving) as ghosts for some reason or another? I have my suspicions, but I can't say for certain what other types of hauntings are, and I can't prove it, either. Still, my heart and my new view of the paranormal world of ghostly happenings make me question; is this all some sort of trick? It wouldn't be the first time the wool's been pulled over the eyes of humanity. We have an enemy and he, unfortunately, is very real. And very, very clever.

According to First Peter 5:8, "Be sober-minded; be watchful. Your adversary the devil prowls the streets like a roaring lion, devouring who he will."

And then this, In Second Corinthians 11:14, "And no wonder, for even Satan disguises himself as an angel of light."

To be blunt, "He (Satan) was a murderer from the beginning, and has nothing to do with the truth, because there is no truth in him. When he lies, he speaks his out of his own character, for he is a liar and the father of lies." John 8:44.

Our world is full of spirits, make no mistake. Remember that we ourselves are spirit beings, having angels and demons wrestle constantly wherever we humans can be found. Read the paper, read the on-line news, watch TV news if you have any doubt. Good versus evil is an old, old story, but doesn't it seem as though our times are the most brutal to date? And that's where my fear for those inexperienced or mislead persons comes to the front.

Though residual haunting might be simply playing back events of the past, it's the other types of haunting that scare me most.

When a spirit or ghost interacts by speaking or seemingly complies with requests, I have to question what's truly happening. Is this a "true" ghost, the spirit of a person or is it something else? Something so clever, so cunning that it knows the "right" answers? Something that knows "only what Aunt so and so knows?" Now we get down to the nitty gritty.

I watched part of a program the other night that frankly made me a bit sick. Yeah, you read that right. I find I can now determine what God intends for me to see on television and what He does not want me to see. But it took a while for me to trust I wouldn't slip back into the dark. Oddly, or not so oddly, it's easy to tell difference.

Two ladies decided to investigate a known haunted house in their town. They'd read what they could find which wasn't much and heard the stories all their lives. That was the extent of their training and preparedness; at least the television audience wasn't told of anything more.

These two very nice women took cameras and recorders into the house, at night, alone. They indeed did seem to capture some fuzzy photos and an EVP of some nature. But what bothered me the most was what they planned to do the next time they visited.

They planned on having a "tea party" for themselves with the ghost as an honored guest, and yes, they were serious.

Well, why not? Surely this is a harmless activity.

Although the stories around this haunting revolve around a child ghost, how do we know for sure this ghost *is* a child? Frankly, the more I dig, the more I am convinced that no ghost is a child ghost. So can these ladies trust that this ghost is a sweet, innocent child? They can't and that's dangerous for the women themselves, and it's dangerous when you consider what might come in, prettily dressed as a little girl or a sweet little boy.

After I switched the program off, I sat there for some time, my mouth was probably open, wondering and stewing for these ladies. They could very well be putting their safety on the line, and they didn't seem to know it. They were admittedly not professionals and didn't have a lot of experience. And even if they had the experience they could not be certain of what they were dealing with. What's more, what if all these fledgling groups and well-meaning people are being used to simply open more doors, more portals between this world and the next?

I recall watching my previously favorite program about ghost hunting a few years ago. This group had tons of experience, but in one episode a team member rebuked a ghost saying, "I'm not convinced you are a child." As I remember, I was a bit put off and felt "sorry" for the poor little child ghost. Looking back now, I'm betting my sympathy was misplaced and that this young lady knew darn well what she was talking about.

When I think of the investigations my little group did, and the times we thought we had a trapped, child ghost to rescue, I shiver. How many times did imposters laugh over fooling us or some other ghost hunting team? How many times did *we* help open a door for something else? Our arrogance in thinking we were doing the right thing makes me more than a bit frightened.

If God allows people to languish here on this earthly plane, why and to what good? Would He really leave a little child here, lost and looking for his or her Momma and Daddy, wandering alone and afraid?

I don't think so. Not any longer. God thinks the world of children, and here are some verses to prove it. Actually, if there were no other verses than the following one, it'd be enough to prove how God loves His babies.

Psalm 139:13–16 "For you formed my inward parts; you knitted me together in my mother's womb. I praise you, for I am fearfully and wonderfully made. Wonderful are your works; my soul knows it very well. My frame was not hidden from you, when I was being made in secret, intricately woven in the depths of the earth. Your eyes saw my unformed substance; in your book was written, every one of them, the days that were formed for me, when as yet there was none of them."

And from Jesus himself, Matthew 18:10 "See that you do not look down on these little ones. For I tell you that their angels in Heaven always see the face of my Father in Heaven." I take this to mean three things. One, the angels who watch over children are so close to God that each and every event that each and every child has on earth is seen by God. Two, no one can fool God or hide from Him. Three, if you harm or cause harm to come to a child, or challenge a child's faith, see the verse below. Our father is specific about that.

Jesus treasured children. He called them to himself and used the little ones as examples of how we all should be. Matthew 18:2–6 "He called a little child and had him stand among them. And he said 'I tell the truth, unless you change and become like little children, you will never enter the kingdom of Heaven. And whoever welcomes a little child, welcomes me. But if anyone causes one of these little ones who believe in me to sin, it would be better for him to have a large millstone hung around his neck and be drowned in the depths of the sea.'"

Jesus wasn't playing. He loves and values children. Does it seem very likely that this same Jesus would leave a child alone in a dark world? It sure doesn't to me. He plainly says to that to enter Heaven, we "must be like little children." For me, that's a case closed, and my heart is secure now that no child is a forlorn ghost, wandering the earth.

It does not convince me, however, that Satan and his bunch of demons can't *pretend* to be a child ghost. What better way to win our sympathy and open a door or two we might otherwise leave shut? What better way to get us to doubt God and throw all kinds of lies at us? Satan knows we love our children, and he uses that love and empathy to his advantage.

Never forget that Satan does not appear with a tail and horns. No, that'd be too obvious. He, as the scripture states, can appear as "an angel of light." He appears as a good friend. He appears to us as that person or thing we wish him to be. And for ghost hunters, he just might pretend to be a forgotten child. But that's not all he can do.

THE VALLEY
OF THE SHADOW

2 CORINTHIANS 11:14–15, "And no wonder, for Satan himself masquerades as an angel of light. It is not surprising, then, if his servants masquerade as servants of righteousness."

Who are his servants? Not just the demons; an obvious answer. We ourselves can fall prey to becoming his servants as well when we knowingly do things that grieve God.

Thing is, he's not alone in his quest to divert our interest away from God. We are told to "test the spirits" and I have to admit, this gave me pause. How are we supposed to do that?

In the book of James 2:19 we're told. "You believe that there is one God. Good! Even the demons believe that-and shudder."

Okay, so Satan, Lucifer, Beelzebub, the Devil, whatever you want to call him and his demon henchmen believe. How does it help us to know that?

Remember, Satan is very, very smart and clever. He has deceived for millennia and shows no sign of stopping. He's too smart to tell us that God doesn't exist. He speaks just enough of a mixture of half truth and lie. We can buy into what he says awfully easily.

The big difference is, from what I've read in the Bible is that his servants won't acknowledge that Jesus is the Lord, the Messiah. They know he's the son of God but they won't, they can't preach that he is nor will they invite people to accept Jesus. They cannot do it! Every spirit sent of God, from God will worship God.

Even the angels don't receive worship for themselves.

In Revelation 19:10 John says, "At this I fell at his feet (the angel who was showing him the future) to worship him. But he said to me, 'Do not do it! I am a fellow servant with you and with your brothers who hold to the testimony of Jesus. Worship God! For the testimony of Jesus is the spirit of prophecy.'"

Satan and/or his servants will be most happy to have our admiration and worship. If you think you're dealing with a spirit, try this out. Ask if Jesus is the *spirit's* Lord. Testify to the spirit and see how it reacts. According to the Bible, it's just about this easy.

The New International Version says: "Dear Friends, do not believe every spirit, but test the spirits to see whether they are from God, because many false prophets have gone out into the world. This is how you can recognize the Spirit of God: Every spirit that acknowledges that Jesus Christ has come in the flesh is from God, but every spirit that does not acknowledge Jesus is not from God. This is the spirit of the antichrist, which you have heard is coming and even now is already in the world" (1 John 4:1–2).

I wish we had remembered this when we were ghost hunting. Oh, we prayed before and after but none of us ever "tested" the spirit. I wonder what would have happened if we had done so during an EVP session? What kind of response might we have gotten? I'll never know.

One other way to test what you can believe is by "the fruit" a spirit bears. In other words, as Jesus said, "No good tree bears bad fruit, nor does a bad tree bear good fruit. People do not pick figs from thornbushes, or grapes from briars" (Luke 6:43).

You can call a tree a Pecan Tree, but if it bears peaches it isn't a Pecan tree no matter what it says.

A spirit can seemingly be from God, but if it acts contradictory to what the Bible says, it simply isn't. If it (the spirit) says Jesus was one good guy and an excellent teacher but not the son of God, don't waste your time any longer. It's a fake and a liar.

Jesus himself allowed temptation by Satan in Matthew 4:1–11. He did this for our sakes, knowing how hard temptation would be for us. He never wanted us to be able to say he didn't understand what we're going through. He does.

Then Jesus was lead by the Spirit into the wilderness to be tempted by the devil. After fasting for forty days and nights, he was hungry. The tempter (Another lovely name for Satan) came to him and said, "If you are the son of God, tell these stones to become bread."

Jesus told him, "It is written: "Man shall not live by bread alone, but on every word that comes from the mouth of God."

Then the devil took him to the holy city (Jerusalem) and had him stand on the highest point of the temple. "If you are the son of God," he said, "throw yourself down. For it is written:

'He shall command his angels concerning you, and they will lift you up in their hands, so that you will not strike your foot against a stone.'"

But Jesus was ready and answered him, "It is also written: 'Do not put the Lord your God to the test.'"

Again the devil took him to a very high mountain and showed him all the kingdoms of the world and their splendor. "All of this I will give you," he said, "if you bow down and worship me."

Jesus said to him, "Away from me, Satan! For it is written: 'Worship the Lord your God, and serve Him only.'"

Then the devil left him, and the angels came and attended Jesus.

We can take comfort in knowing that "the devil left him." In other words, he gave up. We can also take joy in the fact that the angels were just waiting to take care of Jesus. I feel this is true in our own lives. Satan may, and will, mess with us but the angels who "have charge over us" are ready, willing and able to come to our defense and to comfort us.

The verse (New International Version) 1 John 4:4 "You, dear children, are from God and have overcome them, because the one who is in you is greater than the one who is in the world."

This verse gives no quarter and leaves no doubt. Satan is in the house. He is in our world doing the best he can to mess us up, to cause us grief, to urge us to do wrong, to stroke our greatest fears.

He is not, nor shall he ever be, sympathetic, loyal, kind, or even neutral. Let's be crystal clear; he is and always will be our enemy. As our Father's love for us knows no bounds, Satan's hatred of us has no end.

Lucifer/Satan, whatever, urges and encourages our darkest thoughts. If successful, his job is done, but where is he when it all comes crashing down? He's gone. He does not stick around to comfort, to protect, to take the rap, no, he abandons. That look on the accused persons face is total aloneness. They have been left to deal with what they've done on their own. Even then God will, with true repentance on the guilty person's part, comfort his child. Will this change the facts that have already occurred? Will this take away the responsibility of a person's actions? No, but the aloneness is gone and replaced by comfort and strength.

However, the same is true if the devil tempts you but with God's strength and help, you can resist and tell him to shove off in Jesus name. He will abandon you, he has no choice. In this case, his will to ruin your life (any maybe others, too) is left undone. Satan has failed.

The strength the Lord gives us to defeat even Lucifer/Satan is supernatural.

1 Peter 4:12–13, New International Version, says "Beloved, do not be surprised at the fiery ordeal among you, which comes upon you for your testing, as though some strange things were happening to you; but to the degree that you share the suffering of Christ, keep on rejoicing, so that at the revelation of His glory, you may rejoice with exultation."

In other words, don't be shocked at the bad things that will happen in your life. Jesus himself wasn't spared and was tempted, too. "He was despised and rejected by men, a man of sorrows and acquainted with grief." (Isaiah 53:3–4, New International Version of the Bible.)

The son of God "despised and rejected by men?" We all know what happened. Satan leaned heavily on the fears of the religious and political leaders of the day. He convinced them to crucify Jesus though there was no evidence against him. One kangaroo court held at night and in secret, and the deed was done. The only thing Satan didn't get was that it all worked out of love for us. If he had understood what Jesus' death really meant, he would have fought against the death of Jesus. That he did not and does not understand to this day.

Love that will give anything for others is supernatural, paranormal, and given for us to tap into at any time.

Jesus himself said, "Greater love has no one than this, than he lay down his life for his friends." (John 15:13)

Why all of these verses? To show and to remind everyone of the power we have in God. There is no greater power on Heaven, Hell or Earth. We simply remember our privilege to call on the power of God, we remember His love for us, and we ignore anything contrary to this.

A spirit not of God will give itself away. It cannot admit that Jesus is Lord of all; it draws attention away from God and onto itself and it appeals to your ego. I can personally vouch for that.

In my ghost hunting days I enjoyed what others said about how "cool" it was that I headed a real investigating group. I loved to hear how "brave" I was on our investigations. The whole thing slowly became a little play every weekend where I was the star. Our clients leaned on my every word, and I told myself I had the answers. At first, I believed that too.

A CHANGE IN VISION

So, ARE GHOSTS, child or not, real?

My love of the paranormal has been with me as long as I can remember. It still is. The real difference is not so much with me as much as it is a returning of how I believed as a child. In childhood, my faith was strong and pure. It seemed I was instinctively aware of evil and what to avoid. Not until later, after the Ouija board incident that my life became shadowed by darkness.

I followed this dark path for years and well into adulthood. I have already been out told of out what I followed on television, movies, and take out and, put in read in books; even starting my own investigative group. God did not give me comfort while I walked this lane and for that I am grateful. Otherwise I might have never sought out God's will for me.

To know for certain that the God of the universe, the God that made this world and us, loved me enough to reach down and say, "No, child, I don't want you to do this anymore. It's too dangerous," fills my heart with real joy. And it's a joy that still overwhelms me at times. He urged me in that still, small voice until I asked Him what I should do. When I did that, He wasted no time in telling me. And this time the voice was loud and clear.

So here is truth as I believe it. First, let me reiterate that my intent is not to criticize anyone who may happen to believe in ghosts. The spiritual, paranormal world is real and I would never presume to say otherwise. I believe what you have seen and experienced is true. By no means am I calling anyone a liar. Remember, I know better. That's why I've told what has happened to me, my family and my friends. It's all true.

I'm not ridiculing anyone or any group of investigators. However, I can't help but be concerned. The "ghost hunting phenomenon" appears to be taken as lightly as a game in many cases. My new mindset, my belief is that this can be very dangerous.

Perhaps we might have punched a hole through that invisible veil and let in something so bad, so evil that nothing could have even sent it back to the darkness. Maybe He was simply telling me, "You're my child and you have no business with this. You don't know what you're doing."

I believe this was all true in my case. It was so important that God himself gave me an answer so crystal clear that I, the doubter of all time, could not deny it. I grieve that I cannot reach all of you personally and show you how real this is to me. How much I truly believe it.

Now, do I believe that what we see on TV or at the movies is the whole truth and spot on? Do I believe that most ghosts are what they say they are or what they appear to be?

No, I don't. I think we've been lied to and continue to be lied to.

When the message for me to "get out" (pardon me, investigators) came from the Lord, truthfulness washed over me, and I felt like the verse in the Bible where Jesus healed a blind man in the temple and I felt like the verse in Acts 9:18 when Saul, soon to be renamed Paul, was healed from his blindness. "Immediately, something like scales fell from Saul's eyes and he could see again."

It was just that simple. I felt as though I could, in that instant, see through the lies I'd believed. Everything was clear and I was relieved, amazed and somewhat angry. How could I have been so easily tricked? How could anyone believe all this deception, I wondered?

In the past, we've all had practical jokes played on us. Sooner or later, we come to realize we've been had! That feeling is the closest I can come to describing what came over me when the truth dawned on me.

Almost immediately I desperately wanted to warn every ghost hunting group to wake up and start questioning what was happening! To tell the truth I was even embarrassed to admit I'd been so thoroughly deceived. How the enemy must have laughed at our puny efforts to "help." My sheepishness became horror when I began to wonder about the harm we might have done, albeit unintentional. What doors had we opened? Had we turned people away from seeking Gods help?

And why would Satan and his henchmen do such things anyway? Oh, come on, my newly clear mind and heart exclaimed. To fool people is what they do. To turn people away from God is what they *do*, and this plan is nothing short of brilliant.

Not only does all this interest in ghosts turn attention away from the study of God and his paranormal works, it also gives rise to doubts about the afterlife and Heaven.

If little children walk the earth as ghosts, then no one can count on Heaven, can they? Maybe, I can almost hear the doubts, the Bible is not true? Satan is the king of half truths, of lies. He doesn't tell us there is no afterlife, just not the one we were taught to believe in.

And isn't it scary, good fun? Who hasn't enjoyed a good scary movie or story at some point? I dare say most have at one time or another. Take our love of scary, add *real* scary to it and we hardly notice until it's too late. We've been told we don't need to experience the paranormal through others, heck no. We can buy our own equipment and with no experience at all, voila, we're ghost hunters opening all kinds of doors we won't ever know about.

We've all noticed the changes in what we watch and read in the last say, thirty years.

Look what's happened to Halloween, for that matter. When I was a kid back in the covered wagon days we carved pumpkins, Mom made homemade donuts and warm apple cider and we kids took off on our own, at night to go trick or treating.

Now my grandchildren are walked to each door, of a secure neighborhood, by at least one parent or grandparent, aunt or uncle.

That being said if you think our family doesn't celebrate Halloween, we do. We decorate, carve pumpkins, and as I stated, our grandchildren trick or treat. I refuse to lose a day of innocent fun for my grandkids by hiding inside on Halloween. But I know people who call it "the devils holiday."

I refer them to the verse, "This is the day the Lord has made. I will rejoice and be glad in it."

If we hide and stay inside in fear, are we not honoring the devil by doing so?My family and I are of one mind about this.

All right, then, what about these angel stories we read? How about some of these accounts of a beloved grandparent coming back to warn a loved one about something?

Well, first off, I don't think these visitations are by ghosts. Either the spirit has been granted permission by God to deliver this message, or as some believe, an angel is sent in the appearance of the loved one.

Personally, I don't see why an angel would come back disguised as a loved one since they have appeared as ordinary humans many times before and continue to do so still. In some accounts, the angel has appeared as a stranger; not someone known by the witness. Perhaps someone with more knowledge can explain why an angel would need to appear as a loved one but for now I believe God grants, in special circumstances, a visit from a loved one who has passed.

Some will say this is wishful thinking on my part, especially since I spoke and plainly saw my grand-mother in dreams not once, but twice. Some will say it was my grief that manifested into dream visions. Others will say my brother imagined his visit with our grandfather those years ago. Okay, both of those occur-rences occurred in dream states, granted. I intend to study more about that little known state called "dreams" as soon as I'm able.

But what of the phone call my brother received, in the middle of his lunch hour as he sat at his table pay-ing bills? What of my son who heard, "It's okay, kid" during his hospital stay? Who told him, "Michael, Todd's here." as he lay trapped in his car, never losing consciousness? He saw the stars overhead as the cars top was peeled back. He felt the cool January air and smelled the gasoline. He was awake.

What of all the other witnesses who've written of their accounts? Do they stand to profit from these tell-ing? Personally, I don't know of anyone who became rich after telling an angel story. Sometimes one gets called "crazy" and worse for the telling. So, is there something to be gained? Attention, perhaps? For the most part, I don't think so. Personally, I have to believe the stories because after all, my family and I have expe-rienced many of the same things. Years of paranormal history had passed before this book was even a thought.

In re-reading the Bible concerning these matters, I personally became aware that some of my beliefs, some of my understandings may not be correct. I also had to decide which of these understandings were most important.

If we do not walk the earth as ghosts, then what happens to us? Do we go to Heaven or Hell or do we simply "sleep" in our graves, waiting for Christ's return? Until I wrote this book, I thought I knew with all certainty. But one thought keeps running through my mind.

In the long run, we must decide which is more important to us; faith or understanding?

WHAT ABOUT NEAR DEATH EXPERIENCES?

As usual, I turned to the New International translation of the Holy Bible. What did it have to say about death and Heaven? The verses I found surprised me sometimes, even though I truly thought I knew most of them already.

In the Old Testament, 2 Samuel 12:23 King David's infant son has just died. While the child was sick, he prayed, wept and refused to eat. When the child died, his servants were afraid to tell him. David, however, sees them whispering and figures it out. Then he says, "Now he is dead. Why should I fast? Can I bring him back again? I shall go to him but he will not return to me."

Though Jesus, the Messiah, has not been born at this time, obviously King David believed he would be reunited with his child. Not here, but in another place.

Jesus himself said to his disciples, (in John 14:1–4) "Let not your hearts be troubled. You believe in God, believe also in me. In my Father's house are many rooms. If it were not so, I would have told you. I go to prepare a place for you that where I am, you may also be. And you know the way to where I am going."

This is rock solid from Jesus that he is going to "his Father's house" to get places ready for us. He says he will return for us so we can be with him. He uses terms we readily understand even today. Personally, I take heart from this verse. It's to the point and Jesus himself said it. It's what our faith and hope is about, period. We will live again *somewhere* else. And if God Himself is there, our next home will be the very place we've longed for all our lives. That homesick feeling that overwhelms us at times will be gone forever. We'll be home!

Okay, so Jesus says we'll live with him. How will that happen? Will we go to Heaven after we die or do we "sleep" as the Bible calls death until He comes back?

Here are some verses to get you thinking.

In 2 Corinthians 5:6–8 Paul says, "So we are always of good courage. We know that while we are at home in the body we are away from the Lord, for we walk by faith, not by sight. Yes, we are of good courage, and we would rather be away from the body and at home with the Lord."

This seems to indicate that we don't need our bodies to be with the Lord. "Away from the body is to be home with the Lord." is pretty rock solid. However I also ran into this verse in 1 Thessalonians 5:9–11.

"For God has not destined us for wrath, but to obtain salvation through our Lord Jesus Christ, who died for us so that whether we are awake or asleep we might live with him. Therefore encourage one another and build up one another, just as you are doing."

Awake or asleep, huh?

More reading.

1 Thessalonians 4:16–18 "For the Lord himself will descend from Heaven with a cry of command, with the voice of an archangel, and with the sound of the trumpet of God. And the dead in Christ will rise first. Then we who are alive, who are left, will be caught up together with them in the clouds to meet the Lord in the air, and so we will always be with the Lord. Therefore encourage one another with these words."

Some believe, as I always did, that when we die our spirit or soul goes to Heaven. Then when Jesus comes back to Earth (the second coming) he will raise our former bodies new and whole and perfect as his is. This will occur in the "twinkling of an eye" and then those who are alive on the planet will be raised up, caught up, in the air with the Lord and all those whom he has reunited with their bodies.

Still, others believe that our souls "sleep" and that our bodies simply stay in the grave to be raised when Jesus returns. To the dead in Christ, it would seem to happen quickly. Have you ever fallen asleep hard and completely only to awaken the next morning as though you'd only just closed your eyes? I feel it would be like that. To the raised dead, no time would have passed. There would have been no time to "miss anyone" or to be afraid. It would all happen that quickly.

But what of the hundreds or thousands of "near-death experiences?"

I've never personally spoken to someone who has had an NDE (Near-Death Experience) but I'd love to one day.

In all my reading of such events one theme stays the same, no matter whether the final destination was Heaven or Hell. Not one person told of having a choice to stay and hang around here on earth or go through the light, the tunnel, the darkness or wherever they were headed.

Oh, some got to hang around long enough to see their bodies being worked on or their loved ones reactions, but not one said anything about being able to stop the ride and get off. Now, I don't own, I'm sure, every book ever written about the near death experience but I've got quite a library full of just these books. I've read all I can on line, too. And search though I might, I can't find one incident of a person being given the choice to stay here indefinitely.

Please don't confuse this with "coming back" because obviously, these people did and often speak of being told "you can stay here or go back" or even "it's not your time yet." They find themselves back inside their bodies and hardly ever, except in the few "hell" cases I've read about, are too happy to come back to this life. Most find they cannot wait to return there. My father knows of a pastor who died and came back almost angry and depressed! He had wanted to stay so badly but his fear of death was over, never to return. Those who have died to come back may be the only truly fearless persons on the planet.

The near death experience is an amazing, fascinating subject. I intend to keep right on reading. What does it "prove"? Are these people telling the truth? I think they are. Many, when telling their stories, risked ridicule and the stigma of being called "crazy" but they told anyhow. The experiences of these people are never exactly the same, though some are very similar but one thing remains in all, and I just can't ignore that one shared factor.

None, not one, was ever allowed to simply turn down the trip.

Some say that ghosts are people who have passed on and "don't know they're dead" or that this or that person has unfinished business. Therefore, you have a "haunting" and if you can help this person "cross over" they can go on to Heaven. Or wherever.

I used to subscribe to this theory, too and thought I'd helped a few lost souls cross over to the next world. This flies in the face of the near death experiences I've read or heard about.

In the end, we can only look at the evidence we have and in what our hearts believe.

Personally, I don't think we have that option.

THE BIG SLEEP

So WE DIE. Then what?

As I stated before, until now I thought I had it figured out. Sort of.

I believed that when a Christian died, he or she went immediately to Heaven after death. There they would meet Jesus, friends and relatives who had gone on before them. Perhaps they could even "see" us sometimes or at least look in on us down here on Earth once in a while.

As I began to read the Bible to verify these beliefs I got the surprise of my believer's life.

Not all scripture can be interpreted the way I had always believed and not all Christians (gasp) believed the way I always had! Sounds naïve but I really thought every Christian believed the same way about what happens when we die.

Let's look at what the Bible scripture says about what happens to us upon our death. Don't despair as I almost did. We'll get to a place where you'll decide what *you* believe about this most important subject.

Most of the believers I know personally believe as I always have. You die believing that Jesus is the son of God, you confess Him as Lord and when you die, your spirit goes to Heaven. Your body stays in the grave, of course, and when Jesus returns to Earth one day (the second coming) your body is raised, perfectly indestructible. At that time your spirit and your body are reunited and you live in your new earthly body forever.

However, I did have questions. For one thing, why did our spirit and our body have to wait to be reunited at all? Why were we not simply taken up to Heaven, body and all, at our death?

Why are there Bible scriptures that state, (New International version) 1 Corinthians 15:50–53 "I declare to you, brothers, that flesh and blood cannot inherit the kingdom of God, nor does the perishable inherit the imperishable. Listen, I tell you a mystery: We shall not all sleep, but we will all be changed-in a flash, in the twinkling of an eye, at the last trumpet. For the trumpet will sound and the dead will be raised imperishable, and we will be changed. For the perishable must clothe itself with the imperishable and the mortal with immortality."

Okay, "sleep" is used in this verse to describe death. Our earthly bodies "sleep" when our soul leaves it. According to this verse, some of us won't die a physical death but our bodies will be changed and made immortal in an instant. Those who have died the physical death, those in grave, the seas, wherever their bodies lie, will also instantly be reunited with their new, immortal bodies.

Revelation 20:13 "And the sea gave up the dead who were in it, Death and Hades gave up the death who were in them, and they were judged, each of them, according to what they had done."

No body can be so destroyed that it escapes reanimation and judgment. The Bible doesn't stutter about that. This next verse isn't a pleasant one but we can't look at only the good stuff if we want to know the truth.

"But as for the cowardly, the faithless, the detestable, as for murders, the sexually immoral, sorcerers, idolaters, and all liars, their portion will be in the lake of fire that burns with fire and sulfur, which is the second death."

Yikes.

However, remember that this speaks of those who are unrepentant. There is no sin that God cannot forgive of the truly repentant heart. *That* is the good news.

This next verse distinguishes clearly between the mortal body and our spirit or soul. Remember that Jesus rose with a new physical body. He could eat, talk, hear, and appear or leave at will. *This* is what He promises *us*, and there is nothing more supernatural/paranormal than that. Our new bodies will work perfectly and have no constraints of time or place. I, for one, can hardly wait. Also remember that this will happen so quickly, so instantly, that even if we experience physical death of the body, we won't be aware of having waited!

The Bible's authors used sleep to describe this very concept. As I said before, we've all fallen asleep and slept so soundly and deeply that upon awakening, we're amazed the night has passed.

Same thing.

1 Corinthians 15:54–57 says we'll rejoice after our new bodies and our souls are reunited.

"Then, when our dying bodies have been transformed into bodies that will never die, the scripture will be fulfilled; "Death is swallowed up in victory, O Death, where is your victory? O Death, where is your sting?"

Now we need to remember that our soul is not "lost" or floating around somewhere with no particular place to go, as the old rock and roll song says.

Here's some more verse for thought.

2 Corinthians 5:8 "Yes, we are fully confident, and we would rather be away from these earthly bodies, for then we will be a home with the Lord."

Philippians 1:22–23 "But if I live, I can do more work for Christ. So I really don't know which is better. I'm torn between two desires: I long to go and be with Christ, which would be far better for me."

And remember that Jesus himself told his followers he would "come back and get us." In John 14:1–3, Jesus says, "Do not let your hearts be troubled. Trust in God, trust also in me. In my Father's house are many rooms; if it were not so I would have told you. I am going there to prepare a place for you. And if I go and prepare a place for you, I will come back and take you to be with me that you may also be where I am."

If we don't believe what Jesus says than we should just shut the Bible and not read one word of it again. If He is a liar then nothing else matters. I for one believe what He said.

After our bodies and souls are raised to live with Jesus forever the Bible tells us in Revelation 21:4 "He (God) will wipe every tear from their eyes. There will be no more death or mourning or crying or pain, for the old order of things has passed away."

Whichever way, we "sleep" in death or are immediately transported to Heaven, or some combination of both, we are with Jesus. That's enough for me and I must trust in my faith to take care of the details.

The prophet Isaiah, in the Old Testament states, "Behold I will create new heavens and a new earth. The former things will not be remembered, nor will they come to mind."

Sounds good, doesn't it?

HOME SWEET
SUPERNATURAL HOME

SOME CANNOT BELIEVE what an easy process it is to get right with God. Many try to make the whole thing more difficult than it is, and I don't blame them. We're raised to "be good, mind our manners, and use our indoor voices." We're told this is how we become good people and in a way, that's true. But the cold, hard fact is it isn't enough to be a good person.

New International Version of the Bible says in Romans 3:10–12 and 23, "No one is righteous-not even one. No one is truly wise; no one is seeking God. All have turned away; all have become useless. No one does good, not a single one. For everyone has sinned; we all fall short of God's glorious standard."

Sounds dire and hopeless, doesn't it? Not my favorite verse either but don't give up just yet.

Romans 6:23 states, "For the wages (payment) of sin is death, but the free gift of God is eternal life through Christ Jesus, our Lord." Jesus paid our price. See, Salvation isn't really free; it's just been paid for.

Romans 5:8 "But God showed His great love for us by sending Christ to die for us (in our place) by sending Christ to die for us while we were still sinners."

And now this is how easy it is. Only ingredient required is sincerity.

For instance, Matthew 7:21 tells us, "Not everyone who says to me, "Lord, Lord," will enter the kingdom of Heaven, but the one who does the will of my Father who is in Heaven."

My father is fond of saying, "Don't just talk the talk, walk the walk." God knows our heart; He knows our motives, if you will. There's no fooling Him.

Romans 10:9–10 and 13. "If you confess with your mouth that Jesus is Lord and believe in your heart that God raised him from the dead, you will be saved. For it is by believing in your heart that you are made right with God, and it is by confessing with your mouth that you are saved. For everyone who calls on the name of the Lord will be saved."

Now we are at peace with God and our relationship is intact and whole.

Romans 5:1 "Therefore, since we have been made right in God's sight by faith, we have peace with God because of what Jesus Christ our Lord has done for us."

Romans 8:1 "So now there is no condemnation for those who belong to Christ Jesus."

And here's one of my very favorites in Romans 8:38–39, "And I am convinced that nothing can ever separate us from Gods love. Neither death nor life, neither angels nor demons, neither our fears for today nor our worries about tomorrow-not even the powers of hell can separate us from God's love. No power in the sky above or in the earth below-indeed, nothing in all creation will ever be able to separate us from the love of God that is revealed in Christ Jesus our Lord."

That's the whole thing. We're reminded in Ephesians 2:8–9 that our deeds can't do the trick. We cannot work our way to Heaven.

"For it is by grace you have been saved, through faith-and this is not from yourselves, it is the gift of God-not by works, so that no one can boast."

He does expect us to help each other and love each other in deed as well as prayer. For instance in James 2:14–26, "What good is it, brothers and sisters, if someone claims to have faith but has no deeds? Can such a faith save them? Suppose a brother or sister is without clothes and daily food; if one of you says to them, "Go in peace; keep warm and well fed," but does nothing about their physical needs, what good is it? Faith by itself, if it is not accompanied by action, is dead."

However, if you hear someone bragging about their good deeds, well, they have the only reward they'll get for those deeds. In Corinthians, the 13th chapter we're told, "If I speak with the tongues of men and angels but have no love, I am only a resounding gong or a clanging cymbal. If I have the gift of prophecy and can fathom all mysteries and all knowledge, and if I have a faith that can move mountains, but do not have love, I am nothing. If I give all I possess to the poor and give over my body to hardship that I may boast, but do not have love, I gain nothing."

Once a child of God's, you don't want to grieve Him, believe me. We are expected to obey and be examples as children of the living God. When you *do* sin, you won't be at peace until you repent (tell God you're sorry, and mean it) and if you can, make amends. This may mean you have to make some apologies you'd rather not make. Heck, you may even be "right!" Personally, God holds me to this sort of thing very closely.

In one instance I had a bad fight with a co-worker. Can't remember what started it but the tension at work was awful for everyone. And I was miserable. Come to find out, so was my co-worker!

God kept after me to break the ice, knowing it was necessary for ME to make the first move. Man, did I object!

"But I'm right in this!" I protested to God.

His answer? "Your brother is hurting." (This particular friend had experienced the loss of a son.)

I had nothing to say back to that. Our Father was right.

So, one morning I came in, shaking like a leaf, and hugged my friend. We have never quarreled again and yes, he told me he was sorry, too. This co-worker is now a treasured friend.

There have been several more times when God has asked me to be the first to apologize. He has never, ever forced me to do so, but he knows I will do this for Him. And I have never regretted doing so. The joy of a disagreement being reduced to nothing is worth swallowing sticky pride; even when you are right! Our Father doesn't care who's right, he simply wants us to love each other no matter what. (Think of the old Bill Cosby comedy routine; "I don't care who started it!")

Don't think I'm speaking well of myself. How many times I've failed God could fill many books, I'm ashamed to say. He never holds it against me, and I'm grateful. He tells me to get up and try again-even listens to my rants at those times when I just don't "get it." I can practically hear His patience. And sometimes, His amusement.

Just the other day I was sitting on my patio during lunch break, watching my pup play in the leaves. I'd been ranting/praying about something I didn't understand but had finally "shut up" and began to pout.

A baby bird, not sure what kind, landed on the concrete so close to my chair I could have reached out and touched him. Funnier still was how he squawked! The little thing would not move or quiet down! Even my pup's presence didn't faze the little guy. I was beginning to wonder if he was hurt when he cocked his head at me and flew to a nearby tree. But he never quit his rant. I had to laugh. Was this what God heard when I carried on like this little baby? I went back to work with a much better attitude.

I still deal with the loss of my two unborn grand-children. Some days I can't seem to wrap my mind or heart around it. The best I can do is learn to trust God more, even when it seems He's just not hearing us. At times I still tell God I'm angry, especially when I see or hear of one more baby born into our circle of friends. It's hard to swallow jealousy and the "why my kids, Lord?" and try to be joyful for your dearest friends, the same ones who cried with you at each loss.

It's hard knowing that my son and his wife are denied the "certainty" of a problem-free pregnancy no matter what. If they get pregnant again, we'll all be scared and afraid to fall in love with our unseen little one. But we will.

My journey of trust is a long way from over but I'm paddling as hard as I can!

My very favorite verse hangs on my mirror where I have to see it every day, no matter my mood. It's found in Proverbs, the Old Testament, third chapter, verses 5 and 6. Again, this if from the New International Bible.

> Trust in the Lord with all your heart and lean not on your own understanding; in all ways acknowledge Him and He will direct your path.

Should you decide to further explore your own beliefs about the paranormal world, please believe me about one thing, if nothing else?

You can trust God to tell you what is best for you in this area of your life. He won't make you do anything. The message you get will be your own but you have to ask for it first. Please, if you decide to continue on with investigating, make certain and test the spirit as the scripture tells us. That way you'll know that what you receive is true and from God.

I pray you find peace in whatever path you choose. If you ask the Lord before you begin or proceed further, (as I did not) you'll be miles ahead spiritually.

Remember, it's easy.

Open your heart and pray however you are comfortable. No formal words are needed.

First, recognize that you are a sinner, as we all are. It doesn't have anything to do with being a good person. None of us can be so good that Jesus didn't need to die in our place.

Two, ask Jesus to forgive you (HE WILL) and tell Him you want Him to be in your heart.

Three, TRUST that He has saved your soul. It doesn't matter who you were before or frankly, what you did. Lucifer will try to tell you otherwise and make you feel too "bad" to be saved. That is a lie.

Four, Walk the walk, don't just talk the talk. Start over. Don't do whatever it was anymore. When you are weak, call on Him.

Does this mean you have to be perfect?

I guarantee you won't be able to pull that off but if you think you can be, pray some more.

Five, keep in touch through prayer, even when something is beyond understanding. (Remember the verse?)

Try reading the Bible. Personally I would suggest the New International Version because it's easy to understand and is very thoroughly translated. But there are others you may prefer. I'd start in the New Testament and get to know the story of Jesus a bit better. However, Psalms and Proverbs in the Old Testament have helped me at my darkest times as well.

Most of all remember that the God of the universe loves you so much that if He carried a wallet, your picture would be in it. Someone told me that once and I loved the notion.

Don't forget to pray for others and with others. In ways that we can't fully understand there is power in prayer. I can attest to this; I've seen and/or experienced that power.

May God bless you and keep you in the palm of His hand and I hope to see you on the other side.

www.ingramcontent.com/pod-product-compliance
Lightning Source LLC
Chambersburg PA
CBHW060506290526
45791CB00001B/283